ASIA AND THE MAJOR POWERS

Implications for the international order

Robert A. Scalapino

American Enterprise Institute for Public Policy Research
Washington, D.C.

Hoover Institution on War, Revolution and Peace
Stanford University, Stanford, California

AEI-Hoover Policy Study 3, November 1972
(Hoover Institution Studies 37)

Second printing, April 1974

Library of Congress Catalog Card No. L.C. 72-93977

ASIA and the PACIFIC

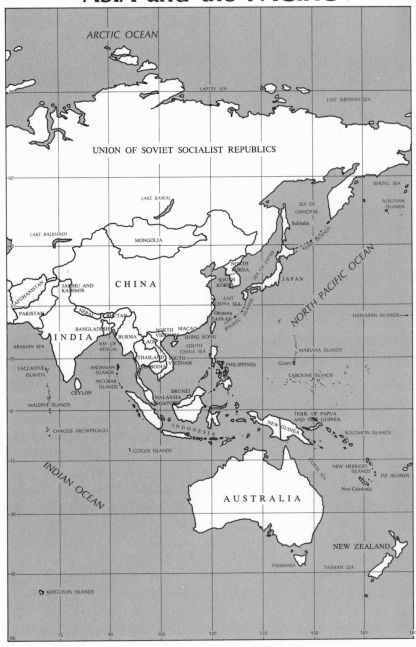

ARCTIC OCEAN

LAPTEV SEA

EAST SIBERIAN SEA

UNION OF SOVIET SOCIALIST REPUBLICS

BERING SEA

LAKE BAIKAL

SEA OF
OKHOTSK

ALEUTIAN
ISLANDS

LAKE BALKHASH

Sakhalin

MONGOLIA

KURIL ISLANDS

NORTH
KOREA

JAPAN

AFGHANISTAN

JAMMU AND
KASHMIR

CHINA

SOUTH
KOREA

SEA OF JAPAN

NORTH PACIFIC OCEAN

PAKISTAN

EAST
CHINA SEA

NEPAL   BHUTAN

Okinawa

HAWAIIAN ISLANDS →

TAIWAN

BANGLADESH

NORTH   MACAO

RYUKYU ISLANDS

INDIA

BURMA

VIETNAM   HONG KONG

LAOS

SOUTH
CHINA SEA

ARABIAN SEA

BAY OF
BENGAL

MARIANA ISLANDS

LACCADIVE
ISLANDS

THAILAND   SOUTH
CAMBODIA   VIETNAM

ANDAMAN
ISLANDS

PHILIPPINES

Guam

CAROLINE ISLANDS

NICOBAR
ISLANDS

CEYLON

BRUNEI
MALAYSIA
SINGAPORE

MALDIVE ISLANDS

TERR. OF PAPUA
AND NEW GUINEA

CHAGOS ARCHIPELAGO

INDONESIA

NEW GUINEA

SOLOMON ISLANDS

COCOS ISLANDS

INDIAN OCEAN

CORAL SEA

NEW HEBRIDES
ISLANDS

FIJI ISLANDS

New Caledonia

AUSTRALIA

NEW ZEALAND

TASMANIA

TASMAN SEA

KERGUELEN ISLANDS

Contents

1
Introduction

Asia has always been an imprecise term. Geographically, it is both more and less than a continent, with boundaries shadowy and shifting. Culturally and economically, it presents a picture of the greatest diversity. Within contemporary Asia, nearly every period of man's evolution and almost every type of his cultural expression are represented. Consequently, people having little in common may live in close proximity to each other. Politically as well, Asia is too heterogeneous to be handled as a unit even when one is dealing on a high level of abstraction.

It is also important to distinguish political Asia from geographical Asia. The two are not synonymous. Hence, in this essay, we shall often speak of the Pacific-Asian area because the major Pacific societies like the United States, Canada, Australia and New Zealand are inextricably connected with Asia both economically and politically.

The Political Configuration of Pacific Asia. Within the Pacific-Asian area, six major societies and five significant regions currently exist. The major societies are the United States, the Soviet Union, the People's Republic of China, Japan, India and Indonesia. The regions of importance are these:

1. *The Pacific,* centering upon the "island states" of Australia, New Zealand, Indonesia, the Philippines and, for certain purposes, Taiwan and Japan, which together with the United States occupy the Pacific physically and depend upon it both strategically and economically.

I am greatly indebted to Ernst B. Haas, Chalmers Johnson, Leo E. Rose and Paul Seabury who read parts or all of this monograph in manuscript form. The responsibility for the contents is naturally mine.

1

The Soviet Union has already entered this area with naval forces, commercial activities, and political ties and is increasingly active there. China is currently involved more minimally, but acquisition of Taiwan could alter this situation dramatically.

2. *Northeast Asia,* with Japan, the Koreas, China and Taiwan constituting its heartland, but with both the Soviet Union and the United States vitally concerned and involved, strategically, politically, and economically.

3. *The Continental Center,* the main actors being China and Russia, and the supporting cast consisting of the peripheral states from Mongolia and the Koreas in the north to Indochina and the Himalayan states in the south.

4. *Southeast Asia,* including both the continental and the island states of the region, stretching from Burma on the west to Australia on the east, from the Indochina states on the north to Singapore and Indonesia on the south, and with all of the major Pacific-Asian states currently involved.

5. *South Asia,* with India its vortex, but with all of the states of the subcontinent included—namely, Pakistan, Bangladesh, Ceylon (Sri Lanka), and the Himalayan states of Nepal, Sikkim and Bhutan; with both Russia and China strongly involved, and the current trend toward lessened American involvement.

It will be noted that these regional units are not mutually exclusive. Many states belong to more than one since some regions overlap. Nor are they fully inclusive since some states of the region are involved in little or no interaction in the supranational arena. Most importantly, each of these regions is characterized by the involvement of the major societies in varying degree and form, whether they be physically in or out of the specific region. Thus, direct major power relations constitute a separate and critical element, capable of being treated apart from the network of regional relations.

An Historical Perspective on the International Systems of Pacific Asia. Let us begin, therefore, by examining the historical development of major society relationships in the Pacific-Asian area, giving special attention to the alliance or security systems that have accompanied these relations.

The modern international system in Asia dates from the beginning of the twentieth century, a period when the leading actors on the international scene were European states. The classical analyses of "Western imperialism" come from this period, with Great Britain serving as the prime example. Great Britain epitomized the sources, nature and purposes of international power at a point when Western Europe was reaching its zenith of global influence. British power developed as a complement to industrial-commercial growth, and its primary purpose was to protect and advance British markets and sources of raw materials. In its opening phases, that power was manifested in private and quasi-private as well as in statist forms. No one need be reminded of the importance of such trading companies as the British East India Company and Jardine Matheson.

Frequently, the British government undertook new commitments reluctantly to preserve old ones, or moved to replace private with public governance, as the rule of trading companies proved inadequate or inoperable. But even in the case of Great Britain, the sources of "imperialism" were not wholly economic. If the British commenced economic development at an early point, they also pioneered in nation-building, that essential political corollary to economic modernization. Nationalism was revealed as a potent and independent instrument of power and instrument of mobilization, both mass and elite. Pride in British institutions and the British way of life promoted a sense of mission that found its manifestations in civil servant, soldier, teacher, missionary, and businessman alike. Great Britain, moreover, produced a surplus of talent as well as of goods. Its civil servants, many of them from a class "destined to rule," combined training, discipline, and skill with a strong sense of *noblesse oblige,* undergoing rigorous sacrifices for the sake of British values and the British Empire.

Great Britain did not stand alone in applying the policies that resulted in the acquisition of colonies abroad. By the close of the nineteenth century, France and the Netherlands held and administered territories in East Asia and the Pacific, far from the motherland. The great colonial empires of this era were built by small states which had come early to the industrial revolution, thus enabling (and propelling) them to translate economic power into political-military power and, in the process, to universalize certain values that had previously been confined largely to the West.

However, another type of Western expansionism, the product of different geopolitical circumstances, was also occurring. The United States and Russia (like China) are continental-mass societies, possessed of a history of self-sufficiency, isolation, and some measure of xenophobia. The expansion of such societies followed a "natural" course, a movement out from the economic-political heartland that gradually encompassed peripheral lands and peoples. In the case of the United States, such expansion took the form of the westward movement and, by the end of the nineteenth century, a continent had been traversed and Americans had moved on, establishing themselves in Hawaii. American expansion, in addition, followed an "unnatural" course as a result of the Spanish-American War. The decision to take over certain territories previously held by the Spanish put the United States in the mid-Pacific and in East Asia as well, with the Philippines becoming a colonial possession of an orthodox type.

The Russians, meanwhile, had retreated somewhat from their eastward movement, which had reached northern California at one point. That movement, however, implanted Russia strongly and—to all appearances—permanently in Central and East Asia, thereby bringing under Russian control vast territories and diverse non-Western peoples. In the north, only a few miles separated Russian and American territory after the U.S. purchase of Alaska. Russia was also a near-neighbor and semi-hostile competitor of Japan, with possessions on the edge of Hokkaido and growing interests in Manchuria and Korea, regions of special interest to Asia's first modernizing state. In addition, the Russian Empire now involved a five thousand mile border with China.

The two forms of expansion outlined above made the five "Western" nations to which we have referred (including Russia) a central part of the Pacific-Asian power structure prior to World War II. Increasingly, Asian international relations had come to be exemplified by the juxtaposition of an active, expansionist West with a passive, defensive Asia. And disputes or changes of power within the Western ranks generally had a greater impact upon international political events in Asia than the activities of indigenous peoples.

In the confrontation of the West and Asia, two radically different concepts of relations among political entities were involved. The West had already established a political system resting upon the nation-state. That unit had become the repository of ultimate power. Consequently, in theory at least, international relations were relations between and among sovereign units, governed by the principles of independence and equality. Reciprocity was expected, as was observance of those international laws that had been formulated relating to conditions of war and

4

peace. In sum, certain of their "progressiveness" and superiority, military as well as economic and political, the major Western states expected an acceptance of a Western-developed and oriented international system.

This system, however, was profoundly foreign to the rulers and peoples of Asia. The "Far East" was still essentially in the pre-nation stage. Primary loyalties were at much lower levels. Authority was highly personalized, status-related and hierarchical. An extensive private government based upon the family and tribe or clan existed alongside of public government, sharing power with it. Thus, concepts of relations among independent states, political units possessed of supreme sovereignty and equality, violated almost all of the precepts that governed historical Asian political relations. In such systems as the tributary system was exemplified the traditional international order of Asia.

The fundamental cause of the recurrent struggles between the West and Asia during the nineteenth century lay in these facts. Commerce served as the vehicle of contact, but basic cultural-political differences between the two international orders that had evolved separately were the ultimate source of friction. In this sense, ideological content has been consistently high in modern international relations within the Pacific-Asian area. Because its most basic challenge was to all traditional institutions and values, the West was an agent of revolution. Indeed, when the age of European domination of the world was over, certain basic values, previously parochial, had become universal —among them nationalism, industrialization, democracy and even the concept of progress. What political elite did not struggle over the right to claim these symbols unto itself as the twentieth century moved toward its conclusion?

Clearly, however, this was not the initial Asian reaction to the Western intrusion. Three major stages were involved in Asia's responses to the West. The first was an effort, uniformly unsuccessful, to reject the West completely, treating its representatives as unwelcome barbarians. A second stage, generally reached by the late nineteenth century, involved the attempt to borrow Western technology while retaining Asian values. At this point, Asian leaders wanted to learn the secrets of Western power, usually to defend themselves against it. When the separation of technology and values proved impossible, a third stage was slowly, often reluctantly, accepted: the quest for a basic synthesis between Western and Asian culture. This included the acceptance of car-

5

dinal Western values, but with these modified to fit the Asian context in which they were to operate. Broadly speaking, that quest continues.

Throughout most of the nineteenth century, the international relations of Asia mirrored the first and second stages of the Asian-Western relation sketched above. Frustrated by the unwillingness of the political elites to accept Western modes of state-to-state relations and infuriated by acts they interpreted as deliberately hostile and deceitful, the Western countries, with Great Britain taking the lead, concluded that their rights could be upheld only by confronting transgressors with superior power. "Traditional Asian rulers respect power, take advantage of weakness" became a recurrent theme, and one that often seemed to be proven by events. By the end of the nineteenth century, the process of applying power had produced a division of the Pacific-Asian area into two parts. Colonial Asia, covering almost the whole of South and Southeast Asia, was under direct Western rule. Independent Asia was largely confined to the north, namely, to China, Korea and Japan. Even for these three countries, independence was precariously held. Through a series of treaties, products of military victories or threats, the West had wrung certain rights of access and control from reluctant Asian rulers.

As time is counted in human affairs, this era proved to be a brief but enormously important interlude. The future, however, was soon signaled by Japan. Within a half century of its forced opening, Japan had accepted the political mores of the West sufficiently to "pass." It thus became the first Asian actor to move onto the international stage as a fully sovereign nation, and this it accomplished in an era of Western dominance. The twentieth century, indeed, was inaugurated by the Anglo-Japanese Alliance of 1902, an alliance that was to have a profound effect upon the international relations of Asia for the two decades it lasted.

Japan, it should be reiterated, became a part of an existing international system, adapting to its ways. Thus, it followed both Western international law *and* the transgressions of that law as practiced by the West. An empire was acquired that initially centered upon Northeast Asia at the expense of China, Russia and, above all, Korea.

2

The Major Powers of Asia

Japan: The Agony of Change

Our examination of the major contemporary Pacific-Asian societies commences with Japan because various insights into the changing character of the Asian international system as a whole can be found in the evolution of its foreign policies. The first important structural changes took place in the immediate aftermath of World War I. That war severely reduced Europe's capacities for global management, and narrowed the circle of those "great powers" able to operate effectively in Asia. Germany and Russia were temporarily eliminated, and even Great Britain, France, and the Netherlands were hard-pressed by events at home and abroad. On the other hand, two non-European powers, Japan and the United States, emerged from the war with enhanced power and prestige.

The Rise of Multilateralism After World War I. The stage was thus set for an alteration of earlier patterns. At the Washington Conference of 1921-22, the highly significant Anglo-Japanese Alliance between the two foremost powers of the West and Asia prior to World War I was set aside in favor of a loosely knit multilateral structure. The latter was outlined in a series of treaties pledging the major European powers, the United States and Japan to protect the territorial integrity of China, to uphold the Asian status quo, to accept naval arms limitations, and to underwrite a political-military equilibrium among the existing major powers.

In many respects, the new structure was a testimony to American concepts and the newly acquired American influence. It rested upon the assumption that the basic values and goals of the participants were similar, that all parties were prepared to play in the international arena according to the same rules. In the event of violations, actual or threatened, only consultation was promised. No sanctions were provided and, in the final analysis, the system rested upon moral suasion. Indeed, these premises were even more graphically displayed in 1929, when the Kellogg-Briand Pact outlawing war was proclaimed. This pact, signed by nearly every nation of the world, symbolized an era in which it was hoped that hard, complex tasks could be accomplished with minimal risks or commitments. The emphasis was upon internal promises and problems, with the role of foreign policy limited as much as possible. Thus, safety was assumed to lie in numbers, and numbers were measured by the solemn pledges collected.

A Rival International System. Meanwhile, however, a rival international order was emerging, an order challenging the status quo and directing special efforts to Asia. In the place of czarist Russia, a new revolutionary state had emerged, the Union of Soviet Socialist Republics. From its early days, the U.S.S.R. made clear its intention of seeking to use the non-West as its prime weapon against the West. Thus, the new Soviet leaders convened a Congress of Toilers of the Far East in early 1922 with the specific purpose of offering an alternative to the Washington Conference. The Bolshevik appeal was an appeal to nationalism, and a united front of patriots was launched to fight the colonial system. Socialism was to be a later achievement.

To carry forth this program, the Soviet leadership created a new international organization, the Comintern, and aimed it directly at the Asian front. Thus, additional dimensions were brought to international relations, with people-to-people and comrade-to-comrade ties being sought apart from, and sometimes in opposition to, state-to-state relations. From this point, it should have been clear that there were more routes into another country than those of military invasion. As noted above, the West had demonstrated this conclusively at an earlier point, but the lesson tended to be forgotten. Now, revolutionaries with radically different objectives (even when they used the old words) had developed new international techniques to support their domestic and foreign policies, and two rival systems confronted each other.

8

The Demise of the Old Order. It was not the Comintern, however, that brought down the first effort at multilateralism in the Pacific-Asian area. Collapse came from within, with Japan playing the critical role. Progressively, Japanese foreign policy moved in directions that challenged the status quo in Asia. The Japanese combined an attack upon Western colonialism with a "forward position" in Northeast Asia. "Asia for the Asians" and "Oppose Communism" served as prime slogans throughout the 1930s. Moreover Japan mobilized a degree of power at home and abroad that dwarfed Comintern efforts and posed a threat not merely to Nationalist China but to the Soviet Union as well.

The weak multilateral system established earlier proved to be ineffectual in dealing with the Japanese assault upon China, and merely faded away. Most of the states involved moved either toward alliance or disengagement. Japan's decision once again was to seek allies outside of Asia in order to promote its policies in Asia. By 1937, it had consummated an alliance with Germany and Italy directed ostensibly against the Comintern and specifically against the Soviet Union. In addition to this alliance, however, Japan greatly expanded its network of ties with diverse Asian nationalists, in preparation for a consolidated attack upon that part of Asia in colonial status.

These various alliances, one formal and directed toward the north, the others informal and aimed at the south, amounted to a new, highly flexible diplomacy that utilized people as well as governments. Japan's drive to launch an East Asian co-prosperity sphere had far-reaching implications. Inevitably, such a diplomacy reached deeply into the internal political structure of various societies, creating counterforces and undermining regimes that could not be toppled directly. In these respects, Japan proved conclusively that the new diplomacy need not be a monopoly of the Communists.[1]

Japanese policies were remarkably successful in the early stages. despite divisions within top Japanese political circles more serious than

---

[1] For some excellent studies in English covering this era of Japanese foreign policy, see Robert J. C. Butow, *Tojo and the Coming of the War* (Princeton, New Jersey: Princeton University Press, 1961); James Crowley, *Japan's Quest for Autonomy: National Security and Foreign Policy, 1930-1938* (Princeton, New Jersey: Princeton University Press, 1966); Herbert Feis, *The Road to Pearl Harbor* (Princeton, New Jersey: Princeton University Press, 1950); F. C. Jones, *Japan's New Order in East Asia: Its Rise and Fall, 1937-1945* (London: Oxford University Press, 1954); and Sadako Ogata, *Defiance in Manchuria* (Berkeley: University of California Press, 1964).

external observers realized at the time. The West, plagued by grave economic troubles, shrank from confrontation and allowed the fragile international system symbolized globally by the League of Nations to be ripped apart. Indeed, Europe increasingly was forced to prepare for a second civil war, as a frustrated, angry Germany reemerged with significant power. The Soviet Union, deeply fearful of a two-front assault, dropped temporarily its savage campaign against established Western governments and pursued united front policies. Understandably, however, the suspicions engendered by past Soviet attitudes and actions continued and these were not alleviated by another bloody purge which did great damage to the Soviet military organization.

Japan also had the problem of two fronts, a problem never fully resolved. To the north, the Soviet Union, despite its increasing preoccupation with Germany, represented a permanent threat. The last Japanese troops in Siberia had departed as recently as 1925. Scarcely 13 years later, Japanese and Soviet troops were again in combat near the Mongolian border, with hundreds of casualties on both sides. In retrospect, this carefully concealed conflict has continuing significance. Whenever the Soviet Union is in confrontation with a major power of East Asia, sooner or later, the troubles are likely to be manifested on its vulnerable northeast borders.

After Hitler's invasion of Russia, however, Japan could gamble that the Soviet problem would be handled effectively by its German ally. The southern front now represented a more pressing problem. There, Japan was confronted by growing unity among Western powers, including the United States, and these powers were in a position to deny it access to vitally needed raw materials and energy sources. In the final analysis, therefore, Japan elected to set the Soviet issue aside, using a nonaggression treaty for this purpose, and to challenge the ABCD (American-Britain-China-Dutch) states frontally. It was a desperate gamble, taken when the alternative seemed to be the collapse of Japan's continental policies—and it failed.

Broad Policy Alternatives for Japan in the 1970s. As Japan confronts the uncertain world of the 1970s, this background continues to weigh upon Japanese consciousness in a variety of ways. The broad alternatives available to Japan today would appear to be five in number: neutralism combined with a minimal political-military role; Pan-Asianism with a premium upon the centrality of a Sino-Japanese accord; Gaullism with an emphasis upon political-military independence and strength; a united front stance amounting to alignment with the "Socialist" forces, especially those of Asia; and a continued alliance with the United States, modified in accordance with certain altered conditions.

These alternatives have been expressed here in "pure" form. In actuality, any Japanese foreign policy of the future is likely to have mixed characteristics, major and minor tendencies, not necessarily totally consistent.

Before examining these alternatives, however, several important considerations pertaining to the Japanese scene must be set forth. At present, there is no consensus within Japan on foreign policy, either on specific issues or basic principles. This is true, moreover, at both elitist and public levels. Among the political elite, the widest conceivable divergencies exist, and even within the dominant Liberal Democratic party, fissures over such issues as China policy have widened in recent years to the point of threatening the party's internal unity.

There is a distinct possibility that Japan will face increasing political instability in the decade ahead, a situation that might well complicate its international role. The effort to reach and hold a consensus is made more difficult by the fact that Japan is one of the most open societies in the world. Contradictory views are thus widely and loudly expressed, seeking to draw the public in radically different directions. As in other open societies, moreover, the media now constitute a problem difficult to exaggerate. In addition to a penchant for the spectacular, the Japanese media display pronounced political biases in many cases, generally "leftist," occasionally shrilly nationalist, normally antigovernment.

Finally, Japan like the United States is a society in the throes of major change, a change stimulated by the extraordinary pace of economic growth in recent decades. Every individual and every institution are being affected. Values, priorities, life style—all are undergoing alterations. Inevitably, foreign policy decisions will be influenced by this rolling revolution.

Neutralism. Let us now turn to the basic issues, beginning with the case for neutralism. This study, it should be noted, makes a distinction between "neutralism" and "nonalignment," two terms that have often been used as synonyms. Nonalignment is defined here as an avoidance of alliance or of intimate ties with any specific nation or group, without

11

this necessarily having political connotations. Neutralism, on the other hand, is used to describe a position with stronger political overtones. Its tendencies are toward political or ideological "centrism," namely an effort to stand midway between what is conceived to be "capitalism" and "communism."

At root, moreover, the neutralist doctrine is based upon the concept of an equidistant multipolarism. This involves the thesis that the major powers or societies are separated from each other in a more or less uniform and equal manner, thus having approximately the same level and character of bilateral relations. Given such a symmetrical pattern of major power relations, it would naturally be easier for a state outside this pattern to adjust its relations with these major powers in a manner similar to the way in which they relate to each other. Neutralist doctrine also rests upon the assumption that ideological and institutional differences need not be of special importance, that a nation like Japan can have relations of equal significance with nations widely separated in these respects.

In its Japanese context, neutralism is generally coupled with an insistence that Japan's role can and should be confined largely to the economic sphere, with political activities restricted in type to those which a truly neutral nation can pursue. Pacifism or a very limited military force involved only in internal defense represents the neutralist position on military policy. It is coupled with the appeal for a multilateral agreement among all of the major powers to guarantee Japan's security, as a substitute for the U.S.-Japan Mutual Security Treaty.

The neutralist position in Japan was historically the property of the Japan Socialist Party and initially it drew heavily upon Nehru's foreign policies in its political and intellectual essence. In recent years, however, the left Socialists who now control the party have moved toward united front policies, although they continue to pay lip service to neutralism. The Socialists are now vigorously anti-American, and strongly pro-Chinese, with such attitudes sharply affecting their policies. The Kōmeitō, Japan's Buddhist-based "Clean Government party," is currently closer to a pure neutralist policy, although as we shall note, it is deeply influenced by Pan-Asian sentiments. Within the Liberal Democratic party itself, some neutralist inclinations can be discerned, especially among younger elements. As to Japanese citizens in general, public opinion polls suggest that as many as one-third have strong incli-

12

nations in the neutralist direction.[2] Recent developments, in particular the prospects of Sino-American rapprochement, have provided the neutralists with additional strength.

Nevertheless, the case against neutralism remains formidable. First, there are serious doubts concerning its basic premise—the existence or possibility of an equidistant multipolarism. There is no indication that the major powers can achieve or maintain symmetrical relations. They certainly are not managing to do so at present, as witness the frigid relations between Moscow and Peking. Perhaps such relations among the major states are not required for the practice of neutralism, or at least for nonalignment by Japan. But in any case, would neutrality serve Japanese national interests?

According to every projection by the Japanese government, the future prosperity of Japan hinges upon maintaining and expanding its primary economic ties with the "advanced" world, particularly with the United States. One-third of all Japanese trade is with America, and that figure is not expected to decline over the next decade. On the other hand, trade with Russia and China is not expected to exceed 6 to 8 percent of total Japanese trade by 1980.[3] It is difficult to see how Japan's economic relations with these three major states can be conducive to an equidistant, neutral stance.

As long as Japan remains an open society, moreover, its political values and in many respects its total culture will have vastly more in common with other open societies than with the Communist states. This

---

[2] In a poll conducted for the USIA by Central Research Services, Inc., between September 1 and 15, 1969, and published in the USIA *Research Memorandum* of June 26, 1970 (p. 18), 29 percent of those interviewed favored a "neutral policy" for Japan, 25 percent favored an "increase of our own military strength," 11 percent favored reliance mainly upon the United Nations, 6 percent union with a regional military group of non-Communist states, and 4 percent reliance mainly upon the United States, with 24 percent responding "don't know."

[3] The economic data used in this study are taken from two sources, *Nenji keizai hokoku* [The annual economic report], a yearly official summary published in Tokyo by the Japanese government, and *Japan Economic Review,* a weekly English-language publication devoted exclusively to economic matters, and containing complete or summarized versions of such official statements as Ministry of International Trade and Industry projections of trade and growth rates up to 1980.

For a recent survey of current data, see *American-Japanese Relations in a Changing Era* by this author, one of a series of The Washington Papers published under the editorship of Walter Laqueur, The Center for Strategic and International Studies, Georgetown University (Freeport, New York: Library Press, 1972).

will be reflected in such fields as art, literature, and the cinema. It will also be of major consequence in educational patterns, life styles, and even in the problems to be resolved. Rapid economic growth has produced urban sprawl, pollution, traffic difficulties, a weakened family system, and many other issues, giving Japan common problems with the advanced world and the need for extensive communications on questions of mutual interest. There is little evidence that comparable ties could exist with the major Communist states in the foreseeable future.

If Japan's economic and political ties with the United States and other parts of the advanced West seem destined to become more intimate, can nonalignment be adopted in the realm of security matters? Almost certainly, this will be a critical issue for Japan in the years immediately ahead. The basic question is likely to come down to this: should security agreements with the United States be abandoned in favor of multilateral guarantees and the establishment of a nuclear-free zone in Northeast Asia?

In practice to date, multilateral guarantees have proved to be the responsibility of no one in case of violation. Can Japan then count upon an absence of violations and the goodwill of all major states? Or should it be assumed that if and when disputes of a serious nature arise, Japan's economic strength will constitute sufficient bargaining leverage, or that it can play one power off against another in the fashion of classic small nation diplomacy?

That there will be disputes, some of them exceedingly difficult to resolve, is clear. They already exist, both with Russia and with China. Of special interest is the Senkaku Islands controversy, because the Japanese are strongly united on this issue and because both the Japanese and the Chinese see it as a nationalist as well as an economic issue.[4] Is Japan prepared to lose such issues because it lacks either sufficient power of its own or such support as a security agreement with the United States could provide?

There is little reason to believe that Japan can count upon wholehearted friendship from either China or Russia in the near future,

---

[4] The Senkaku Islands lie between Okinawa and Taiwan and, according to the Japanese, have been historically attached to the Ryukyus. Recently, off-shore oil deposits were discovered, increasing the islands' potential value. Both Peking and Taipei have now claimed the territory. In response, Japanese official and unofficial statements have been overwhelmingly insistent upon Japan's rights, with an indication that these would be defended militarily, if necessary.

14

despite recent progress in normalization efforts. Existing sentiments will continue to be deeply impregnated with suspicion, rivalry, and hostility, products of both the historical legacy and the recent economic explosion underway in Japan. As we shall see, one of Peking's central objectives is to contain Japan, politically and militarily, and to prevent any close ties among Japan, South Korea, and Taiwan. A persistent Chinese theme of recent years has been to emphasize the danger that Japanese militarism will follow inevitably from Japan's new-found economic power.

The establishment of formal diplomatic relations between Japan and China—which has just occurred, largely but not wholly on China's terms—may create a climate of improved state-to-state relations and reduce Peking's heavy barrage of criticism against Tokyo. It would appear that China's deep current hatred of the Soviet Union, together with its desire to prevent Japanese support for an independent Taiwan, induced Peking to make certain modifications in its earlier terms for the normalization of Sino-Japanese relations, primarily with respect to economic issues. Thus, the question of reparations was not raised and no formal obstacles were placed in the path of continued Japanese trade with Taiwan. In exchange, however, Japan agreed that normalization proceeded from a "full understanding" of China's three principles, including the principle that Taiwan is a part of the People's Republic of China, and accepted the added notation that the government of Japan "respects" Peking's stand. In addition, the joint communique appeared to remove the legal validity of treaty relations between Japan and the Republic of China on Taiwan by stating, as its first point, that "the abnormal state of affairs . . . [which can be interpreted to mean the formal state of war between Japan and China] is declared terminated" as of the publication date of the communique (September 29, 1972). Hence, in return for certain economic concessions by China—the permanence of which, with respect to trade, remains to be tested—Japan made the bulk of the legal and political concessions. Consequently, certain basic problems are likely to persist, making Sino-Japanese relations complex for the foreseeable future.

Russia too, after a long period of supporting harsh policies toward Japan and showing only limited interest in improved relations, has recently indicated an increased desire for rapprochement, primarily because of its growing concern over China. Thus, under current conditions, Japan may be able to play off the major Communist states against each other in some degree, using economic power as bargaining leverage. Among other things, however, this will require the most careful timing. For example, Russia has given some indication of being both worried and angered at the rapidity of Sino-Japanese normalization. In the end, bargains are likely to be reached on the basis of cool, non-sentimental calculations of national interests and prevailing considerations of rival capacities and alternate risks, as the just concluded Sino-Japanese agreement on normalization indicates. If Japan stands alone and disarmed, it must be prepared to bargain from weakness with nations now firmly committed to bargaining from strength.

Pan-Asianism. Does Pan-Asianism offer more than neutralism? It has an emotional appeal to a people that have had some portion of their identity ripped away by the industrial revolution. Racial consciousness remains very strong in Japan, as does pride in an ancient civilization. Moreover, the strongest cultural ties in Japan's past are with China. Thus traditionalists and avant-garde radicals can unite in insisting that Japan must have special relations with China and, through China, with the world of Asia.

China is a supremely important issue in Japan for a great mixture of reasons, but the ratio of sentimental and basically irrational arguments to rational ones is remarkably high. Although public opinion concerning the Chinese Communist regime has proved to be volatile in recent years, and although economic opportunities would appear limited, over one-third of the respondents in one recent poll said that Japan's closest ties should be with the People's Republic of China, partly, one may presume, because this was considered a natural, historically sanctioned development.[5] Indeed, this constituted a significant pressure upon the new Tanaka government to reach an agreement with Peking quickly— even at a considerable cost. No comparable pressures, it might be noted, operate with respect to the Soviet Union.

---

[5] For data on polls taken in September 1969 and December 1971, see *Asahi Shimbun*, January 3, 1972 (pp. 1, 7). In these polls, the question was posed: "With which foreign country should Japan maintain the closest friendly relations in the future?" In September 1969, 40 percent of those polled answered, "the United States," only 10 percent, "China," whereas in December 1971 the figures were 28 percent and 33 percent, respectively. Obviously, care should be used in giving weight to such data. The December 1971 poll was undoubtedly influenced by trends after mid-1971, notably the Nixon trip to Peking and the crisis in Japanese-American economic relations. The results should be seen only as a trend, not as a precise measurement of sentiment.

In a sense, Japan has already accomplished an important portion of its earlier Pan-Asian objectives. A new "co-prosperity sphere" exists throughout Southeast Asia, with Japan playing the dominant role. Even in the northeast, Japan's economic intercourse with South Korea and Taiwan is extensive—and with China itself it is greater than that of any other foreign state. When Pan-Asianism is pushed too far, however, it defies reality. Japan is an Asian society; but, as we have indicated, it is also an advanced industrial society and this fact gives it greater links with nations like the United States than with either China or Indonesia. Even the Japanese people are cognizant of their extensive links with the "developed" world in reflecting upon which nations they most and least admire. Ever since opinion polling on this question began, those most liked have been exclusively Western: Switzerland, Great Britain, France, and the United States. Those least liked have been neighboring "Asian" states: the Soviet Union, China, and Korea.[6] Pan-Asianism will continue to have some validity and considerable emotional appeal, but it cannot serve as the cornerstone of Japanese foreign policy.

Gaullism. Is Gaullism appropriate to Japan's needs? Let us define Gaullism as a policy of asserting perceived self-interest via an independent stance, risking the alienation of allies, real or potential. In it, the quotient of nationalism is very high, and a concentrated effort is made to raise the state's prestige and power or role by all available means—economic, political, and military. An acute consciousness of such matters as status and role is present, and slights in these respects are quick to be felt.

The emotional appeal of such a policy to a certain Japanese constituency cannot be denied. Nationalism is now moving forward in Japan at an accelerating rate. After years of subordination to external authority and a low posture before the world, the Japanese are exhibiting a rising sense of self-confidence and pride. At the same time, complex factors in Japanese culture make alliance difficult and self-sufficiency attractive.

In addition to the psychological factors which abet it, Gaullism rests upon two premises. First, at some point in the future, Japan will face an external threat, or will be subjected to repeated blackmail and

---

[6] See the Jiji Press polls as cited regularly in the USIA *Research Memorandum,* a monthly publication originating from the United States Information Agency, Washington, D.C.

see its own interests slighted or ignored—as long as it is weak and dependent. Second, the American commitment is no longer credible since the United States will increasingly be involved in its internal problems and will withdraw from Asia.

Logically, Gaullism points toward the acquisition of nuclear weapons. Here, in addition to the arguments concerning Japan's authority, certain military questions are posed. Of what advantage would a conventional force be, of whatever size, against a nuclear China or Russia? And are not the modern weapons which Japan is now acquiring, the latest submarines and aircraft, designed to carry nuclear weapons?

These questions are not easily answered, but the real problem lies with those questions that are not usually asked. Has Gaullism really worked in the nation of its origin? France under de Gaulle sacrificed much, including the goodwill of erstwhile allies, to acquire nuclear weapons and pursue an "independent" foreign policy. But these sacrifices gave France neither major power status nor greater security. Nor does the evidence suggest that foreign markets can be protected by military means. Are they not more likely to be jeopardized in a number of instances by the fear of a revitalized Japanese militarism? Finally, nuclear war seems scarcely believable among any combination of major powers, but is it not totally incredible to contemplate in the case of Japan—a nation of one hundred million people occupying a space no larger than California, crammed into unending metropolitan complexes?

Gaullism, nevertheless, will continue to have a strong appeal and, in certain forms, it will probably find expression in future Japanese foreign policy. This does not necessarily mean, however, that Japan will acquire nuclear weapons. The odds are strongly against that development at present. The nuclear option will be kept open, under the formula of "nuclearization minus two"—meaning that if necessary, Japan will be able to acquire such weapons in two years. Unless a greatly increased perception of threat develops, however, or unless American credibility largely disappears, the furthest reaches of Gaullism are likely to be avoided in Japan.

United front. Another extreme policy would be that of united front, a conscious commitment by Japan to the "socialist" cause. Little time need be spent on exploring this possibility because it is extremely unlikely. Only a domestic revolution that brought some combination of left Socialists and Communists to power could make such a policy feasible. Even then, the differing commitments of Socialists and Communists would make a policy of this type complicated as long as the Sino-Soviet cleavage continues. The Japanese Communists are presently extremely anti-Mao, while the Socialists are vastly closer to Peking than to Moscow. But while a united front policy is not conceivable as the dominant line, it will continue to have influence on the "neutralist" position.

Modified alliance. The final alternative would be to continue the alliance with the United States, modifying it in certain ways to conform with the times. The case for such a policy has already been suggested: the vital importance of U.S.-Japanese economic and cultural ties to both countries, the political bonds between two open societies, and the common interest which each state has in a political-military equilibrium in Asia, particularly Northeast Asia.

To explore further the factors favoring or militating against this policy, however, requires that we examine the likely goals of Japanese foreign policy in the decade ahead. Perhaps these can be set forth as follows: First, economic concerns will continue to be paramount, given the population, resources, and current expectations with which this state must deal. Thus, foreign policy must serve to protect and advance Japan's access to markets and sources of raw materials and energy supplies. Since Japan hopes to expand its economic activities everywhere, it would benefit greatly from reduced global tensions, a lowering of ideological confrontations, and the maximum degree of openness—both economic and political—on the part of other states. It is absolutely essential, in any case, that the "advanced" world, particularly the United States, remain open and healthy.

These objectives will also be forwarded if a broad political-military balance in Asia is preserved, whether Japan participates actively in such an effort or not. Its economic access to critical areas such as Southeast Asia hinges in some measure upon developments in this respect. Moreover, security factors are involved. In particular, Japan has a major stake in the preservation of the Republic of Korea, and its stake in an independent Taiwan may also be considerable, despite the recent concessions on this issue.

In the light of these interests, a modified alliance with the United States would seem to be the most logical broad alternative among those available for Japan. Under such a policy, to be sure, Japan would take an increasing number of independent positions and would insist upon full consultation as well as a reciprocity of treatment equal to its acceptance of responsibility.[7]

Rational calculations, however, will not necessarily prevail. Emotional factors are playing a substantial role in United States-Japan relations at present, and generally a negative one. The treatment of economic issues during recent years in an ad hoc fashion, midst mounting crisis, coupled with the absence of prior consultation on such vital issues as President Nixon's visit to China, have created an atmosphere of suspicion and hostility in many quarters. The sense of having been relegated to secondary importance, even of having been betrayed, has mounted in Japan. This, coupled with the fear of isolation, has exacerbated Japanese nationalism while at the same time turning it frequently in an anti-American or "neutralist" direction. Despite a great store of common interests, the American and Japanese peoples are products of radically different cultures and, to each, the concept of alliance is accepted only with difficulty. Thus, the years ahead are likely to test to the utmost the viability of the American-Japanese alliance in a changing Asia.

The People's Republic of China: A New Asian Power

The contrasts between Japan and the People's Republic of China (P.R.C.) today are striking. These two societies, with certain historic cultural roots in common, now diverge in the timing of their modernization efforts, in the central characteristics of their economic and sociopolitical systems, and in the most basic principles that make up their citizens' value structure and way of life. The old affinities based upon cultural linkage are largely remembrances of things past.

---

[7] For other stimulating expositions of Japanese-American relations published recently, see Zbigniew Brzezinski, *The Fragile Blossom* (New York: Harper & Row, 1972); Gerald Curtis, ed., *Japanese-American Relations in the 1970s* (Washington, D.C.: Columbia Books, 1970); Irwin Isenberg, ed., *Japan: Asian Power* (New York: H. W. Wilson Co., 1971); Herman Kahn, *The Emerging Japanese Superstate: Challenge and Response* (Englewood Cliffs, New Jersey: Prentice-Hall, 1970); and the hearings chaired by Congressman John Culiver, Subcommittee on U.S. Foreign Economic Policy, Committee on Foreign Affairs, House of Representatives, 92nd Congress, 1st session, November 2, 3, 4, and 8, 1971.

Central Components of Chinese Foreign Policy. What are the foreign policy alternatives currently available to China? First, we should note those central ingredients likely to be a part of any Chinese foreign policy: nationalism, Marxism-Leninism-Maoism, and tradition. Of these, nationalism has surely been the dominant element thus far, and there is little reason to anticipate a change in this respect.

In many ways, the P.R.C. has behaved in the international realm precisely as one would expect of a large society emerging after a lengthy period of minimal and uncertain contacts with the world. Its leaders have placed a very high premium upon nation-building, seeking to instill in each citizen a fierce patriotism. Yet at the same time, they have been cognizant of China's manifold weaknesses and backwardness, and they still bear the scars of having long been part of a sick, impotent state. All of these factors have helped to shape the nationalism that is so manifest in the attitudes and policies of the contemporary Chinese Communist elite.

Thus, China has been engaged in a series of actions designed to strengthen and defend its borders. Some of these actions have involved alliances or close relations with states having very different political systems. On the other hand, nationalism has also been the prime factor in splitting China apart from the Soviet Union with which it supposedly shares a common ideology and political system. Indeed, nationalist issues between the two Communist giants have risen steadily in importance in the decade since 1961.

Given China's serious internal problems, it is not surprising that most Chinese policies have been defensive in character, and that considerable caution has been exhibited about coming into confrontation with either of the "superpowers," especially since the Korean War. Nevertheless, Chinese nationalism has also manifested itself in pressures upon certain small states on China's peripheries that must be considered offensive, not defensive, in nature.[8] Moreover, China has main-

---

[8] It is interesting to note that even with respect to North Korea, the Chinese have exercised strong pressures on occasion. For example, in 1956, the Chinese together with the Russians put heavy pressure upon Kim Il-sŏng in the course of an internal power struggle in P'yŏngyang; again, in 1967-1968, open attacks upon North Korean policy and leadership emanated from official and quasi-official Chinese sources. Since 1969, however, Chinese-North Korean relations have significantly improved.

The extent of Chinese involvement in the internal affairs of various Southeast Asian states and, more particularly, in support of various Southeast Asian Communist parties is a matter of debate, and some of the critical facts are diffi-

tained and even strengthened in some instances its ties with overseas Chinese communities, another manifestation of the way nationalism, irrespective of its political coloration, continues to be linked to profound racial consciousness in Chinese political culture.[9] In addition, the determination to acquire a major military arsenal that includes nuclear weapons, coupled with the assertion by no less a source than Chou En-lai that China has a "special responsibility" in Asia, must be set alongside the oft-repeated statement that China has no desire to become a superpower. The nationalist urge in China today—both at elitist and mass levels—is as strong and as powerfully cultivated as it has been at any point in the long history of that massive society.

Both the style and the substance of Chinese foreign policy, however, reveal the continuing influence of ideology. In all controversies abroad, and especially those with the Russians, Peking is forced to define the issues as involving a struggle between "true" and "false" Marxists. Orthodoxy and heresy, indeed, become issues unto themselves. Moreover, the P.R.C., while adopting as its central line the thesis that revolutions must be conducted with primary reliance upon indigenous resources, also acknowledges the responsibility of any true Marxist party to forward the cause of international proletarian solidarity.

---

cult to obtain or subject to differing interpretations. Unquestionably, the P.R.C. has raised and lowered its comrade-to-comrade relations, depending upon time and circumstances. Certain policies worrisome to the governments of this region, however, have been constant, notably those of providing residencies in Peking to key Southeast Asian Communist leaders, supplying some arms and training to certain guerrilla elements, and permitting clandestine radio transmitters purporting to be the voice of various "liberation" movements to operate on Chinese soil. It is extremely difficult to interpret these actions (applying variously to Indonesia, Malaysia, Thailand, Laos, and Burma) as purely "defensive" in character.

For differing interpretations of Chinese policies in Southeast Asia, and toward the Communist movement of this region, see Bernard K. Gordon, *The Dimensions of Conflict in Southeast Asia* (Englewood Cliffs, New Jersey: Prentice-Hall, 1966); Melvin Gurtov, *China and Southeast Asia—The Politics of Survival* (Lexington, Massachusetts: D. C. Heath & Co., 1971); Harold C. Hinton, *Communist China in World Politics* (New York: Houghton Mifflin Co., 1966); Peter Lyon, *War and Peace in Southeast Asia* (London: Oxford University Press, 1969); and Robert A. Scalapino, ed., *The Communist Revolution in Asia,* 2d ed. (Englewood Cliffs, New Jersey: Prentice-Hall, 1969).

[9] After President Nixon's visit to China, one of the P.R.C.'s first moves to establish extensive contacts within the United States involved Americans of Chinese ancestry. Significant numbers of American-Chinese were invited or allowed to come to China, with few if any questions raised about their political backgrounds, a situation quite different from that applying to other Americans. Many American-Chinese, moreover, were permitted to visit their ancestral homes while in China.

Indeed, Peking has pursued the three-tiered diplomacy that is described above as associated with the advent of Communists to power: state-to-state, people-to-people, and comrade-to-comrade. It has been possible to change the mix from time to time, depending upon the circumstances and the country involved. Thus, Sino-Burmese relations are characterized at one point by Peking's condemnation of Ne Win as a "fascist" and by extensive support for the White Flag Burmese Communists, and at a later point by a rekindling of state-to-state relations (with Ne Win a state guest in Peking (August 1971) but with certain top Burmese Communists still quasi-permanent residents in Peking and occasionally photographed with Chinese leaders, in part, no doubt, to signal to Rangoon the availability of another Burmese leadership).[10] In both people-to-people and comrade-to-comrade diplomacy, the ideological content is likely to remain high.

Nor is tradition—including the tradition of the distant past—dead. In many respects, "barbarian management" is still the preoccupation of China's leaders, with tributary relations a continuing goal. Concepts of sovereignty and equality among nation-states are still forced to coexist with older concepts of suzerainty and China as the axis around which the relations among Asian peoples should revolve.

Policy Alternatives of the 1970s. Against this background, what are the broad foreign policy alternatives available to the People's Republic of China as the 1970s commence? Neutralism, particularly neutralism-pacifism, is not a viable alternative for China at present. In the first place, neutralism evokes strongly antagonistic reactions from China's leaders because it runs counter to the Marxian insistence that good Communists cannot remain neutral on specific issues or in their general posture in the world. Also, as is well known, China has embarked upon a major program of military expansion and modernization

---

[10] Nor was Ne Win completely satisfied with the results of his Peking visit, if reports obtained from reliable sources in Rangoon in mid-1972 are correct. It is asserted that Ne Win expressed the hope to Premier Chou En-lai that, with state-to-state relations beween China and Burma improved, further aid to forces destructive to Burma's political order would be discontinued, and that the Chinese premier's response was a bland, "China never interferes in the internal affairs of another nation." A few months later, in November-December 1971, some 2,000 rebel troops under White Flag Communist leadership, armed with AK-47s and other relatively sophisticated Chinese-derived equipment, launched a very serious attack in the northeast, and almost succeeded in seizing a provincial capital.

involving both nuclear and conventional weapons. Costly though this program is, it is inconceivable that the Chinese would be prepared to abandon it and take their chances as a disarmed nation living cheek-by-jowl with the Soviet Union—quite apart from the ideological strictures that make pacifism a "petty bourgeois" weakness.

A minimal foreign policy. It is legitimate, however, to speak of a minimal foreign policy, even one with a strong isolationist content, as an alternative for the P.R.C. Giving lip-service to internationalism is every Marxist's duty. Investing a sizable proportion of funds, personnel and efforts on international operations, official or unofficial, is another matter, particularly if it involves very considerable military-political risks.

China presently faces as massive a task as that confronting any contemporary state. Some 700-800 million people, their numbers still increasing, must be raised from the grinding poverty that now encompasses the great bulk of them if China is to bear comparison with the other major nations. Even if this task is given the most concentrated attention, the prospects for success must be regarded as uncertain and the time required will have to be measured in decades, with periodic setbacks likely. Under these circumstances, can China afford to direct major energies toward a demanding, expansive foreign policy? Would this not defy the priorities made natural for China by the situation now prevailing, and risk internal crises of major proportions?

And would it not also challenge natural proclivities? Historically, the Chinese have generally been characterized by an inward orientation. China has a great culture that is at once comprehensive and exclusivist. To enter this culture in full measure without a commonality of birth and race has been extraordinarily difficult. Is there reason to believe that the Chinese, who have managed to carry with them a considerable sense of self-sufficiency and superiority even while passing through extremely dispiriting experiences, could summon up the qualities of mind, will and commitment necessary to the success of a new, "forward" foreign policy?

One cannot accept this alternative, however, without a careful exploration of the factors militating against it. A state committed to Marxism-Leninism and cultivating with all of its resources a fervent nationalism cannot be a state easily committed to a minimal foreign policy. At the very least, the Marxist-nationalist and isolationist positions

24

involve a strong element of paradox and, hence, represent positions that cannot easily be made to coexist with each other.

Even in the historic past, China experienced eras of empire, when expansionism was the order of the day. Nor is it accurate to relegate militarism to an insignificant role in the creation and maintenance of the historic Chinese order in East Asia. There were Chinese military heroes long before the era of the Communists.

Here, however, we must be concerned primarily about the contemporary scene. Clearly, the picture is a mixed one. At various points in the recent past, the People's Republic of China has shown an interest in going far beyond border maintenance policies. It has competed for leadership of the so-called "third world movement," engaged in aid and technical assistance programs not merely in Asia but also in Africa and the Middle East, provided training and military hardware for guerrillas from Burma to the Congo and, most importantly, penetrated deeply into the politics of such nations as Japan via people-to-people diplomacy. To be sure, certain of these policies, notably those involving military or economic aid, have been circumscribed by the profound weaknesses of China in these opening decades of the new order. The deficiencies, however, are of capacity, not of will, if we may believe party spokesmen.[11]

Moreover, internationalism itself can be defended as a necessary defensive policy. At the height of the Cultural Revolution, as is well known, the so-called left, temporarily in control, succeeded in isolating Peking from almost all external ties of significance. There followed the traumatic events of 1968-1969, starting with the Soviet invasion of Czechoslovakia, Brezhnev's enunciation of the doctrine that no state shall be permitted to leave socialism, and the growing crisis in Sino-Soviet border relations, climaxed by a scarcely veiled threat on the part of the Russians to use nuclear weapons if necessary to counter Chinese actions. Suddenly, Peking was caused to realize the folly of entering

---

[11] For recent surveys of Chinese foreign policy in addition to those already cited, see Gavin Boyd, "China," in Wayne A. Wilcox, Leo E. Rose, and Gavin Boyd, eds., *Asia and the International System* (Boston: Winthrop Publishers, Inc., 1972), pp. 2-31; Harold C. Hinton, *The Bear at the Gate: Chinese Policymaking Under Soviet Pressure* (Washington, D.C.: American Enterprise Institute, 1971); J. D. Simmonds, *China's World—The Foreign Policy of a Developing State* (New York: Columbia University Press, 1970); and "China's Policies in Asia and America's Alternatives," Tang Tsou, ed., *China in Crisis,* vol. 2 (Chicago: University of Chicago Press, 1968).

negotiations from a position of weakness, with only the most limited external relations. From this realization flowed new interest in entering the United Nations, reopening and expanding diplomatic contacts throughout the world, and, above all, exploring a more flexible policy with the United States. These policies, it should be noted, were defended at home as necessary "defensive" measures against the Soviet (and Japanese) threat.[12]

When do defensive policies become offensive? When does a military program based upon an essentially defensive psychology yield offensive capabilities as well? It has frequently been argued that Mao's adamant rejection of a military program based upon closer interaction with the Soviet Union, as well as his emphasis upon people's wars, the total mobilization of the entire country and the full exploitation of guerrilla tactics, testifies to the defensive orientation of the People's Republic of China. This is generally true—at present. Mao and those of like mind distrust the Russians profoundly, and seem determined to go it alone, militarily and in other respects. It is clear that they must think initially in defensive terms and see the U.S.S.R. as the primary potential opponent at this time. In the foreseeable future, China cannot conceivably reach military parity, especially in nuclear weapons, with either the Soviet Union or the United States. Nevertheless, as Chinese conventional forces are modernized—a program underway—and as nuclear weapons become operative, China will have a formidable offensive capacity against any but the two superpowers.

Alliance. A second foreign policy alternative would be the establishment of a policy of alliance—an alliance that would support China's economic, political and security needs or desires. The Chinese Communists began their rule by reaching toward such a policy, in the form of a close alliance with the Soviet Union. That alliance did indeed have a marked influence upon many aspects of the New China during the first years of the Communist rule.

Could the Sino-Soviet alliance be reestablished at some future point? Such a possibility cannot be rejected out of hand, despite the

---

[12] The recent issues of *Peking Review*, the official weekly journal intended for international consumption, make fascinating reading, because the articles selected for publication there allow one to grasp the changing moods and emphases that have characterized Chinese foreign policy in the past twenty-four months. For more general theoretical justifications, of course, one should consult *Hung Ch'i* [Red flag], the party's monthly theoretical journal.

fact that the chances seem remote at present. Clearly, there would be extraordinary advantages to both sides if current hostilities could be replaced by cooperation. The costs involved in keeping huge military forces on the border, as well as the separate development of military weapons, are tremendously burdensome, especially to China. The political losses suffered by both sides in the no-holds-barred struggle for influence in the revolutionary world have also been incalculable. The reputation of both parties has been besmirched, and the secrets revealed have cast a pall of gloom over the entire Communist world.[13] Moreover, the abrupt severance of scientific and technological aid has proven to be exceedingly costly to China, with no real replacement yet having been obtained.

These are but the most obvious reasons why Sino-Soviet rapprochement must have a continuing attraction to at least some individuals within both states. There is good reason to believe that, at certain points, the issue of relations with the Russians has been a deeply divisive one within the uppermost Chinese ranks, although the Maoist theme that many of those purged have been "Khrushchevites" or "lackeys of a foreign power" is undoubtedly a gross exaggeration. In the aftermath of Mao—and of current Soviet leaders—the possibility of improving Sino-Soviet relations could well become a recurrent issue, both in Peking and in Moscow.

The obstacles to a revitalized Sino-Soviet alliance, however, are formidable. The long history of Russian-Chinese relations has been dominated by suspicion and hostility, a legacy that exacerbates tendencies within both countries toward aloofness and xenophobia. These two peoples, profoundly different in culture, have been forced to inhabit the heart of the Eurasian continent together, with an ever closer physical relationship since the Russian absorption of portions of central Asia. On both sides, racial sentiments run strong and the cultivation of nationalism in recent decades has heightened such sentiments. Put in the broadest terms, the U.S.S.R. and the P.R.C. currently represent two nation-states which seek to share a common ideology but have profound differences with respect to the timing of their revolutions, the stage of their economic development, and the degree of their military power.

---

[13] The classic work in English on the Sino-Soviet dispute in its earlier phases is Donald Zagoria, *The Sino-Soviet Conflict, 1956-1961* (Princeton, New Jersey: Princeton University Press, 1962).

These differences make inevitable very different interpretations of what policies, foreign and domestic, constitute the national interest—interpreted, of course, by each state's political-military elite.[14]

Some degree of normalization in Sino-Soviet relations is conceivable, even probable. Neither side could possibly desire war, since such a war could not be won and its costs would be incalculable. A mutual advantage, therefore, exists in seeking some modus vivendi and a reduction in tension, although both the Chinese and the Russians have shown themselves to be tenacious, stubborn bargainers. In any case, however, even with new leaders, a Sino-Soviet alliance of the type initiated earlier now seems highly unlikely. Not only have all of the old suspicions and hatreds been rekindled, but also both states are presently engaged in ever more complex relations with the non-Communist world, relations encompassing the economic, political and strategic fields. This development alone makes the reestablishment of the old Sino-Soviet order more difficult and less desirable from the perspectives of either Peking or Moscow.

Is an alliance with the other superpower, the United States, a likelihood? Little time need be spent in contemplating this possibility. Recent events have shown that two nations holding as radically different values and policies as China and the United States can reach an improved level of communication and even some degree of accommodation when it seems in the self-interest of each to do so. This type of development we label "normalization." There is a vast difference, however, between normalization of relations and an alliance.

One could envisage a true American-Chinese alliance only under dramatically different conditions from those which now prevail in Asia and in the world, conditions involving an external threat against both from the same perceived source, or sources. Since this is most unlikely, a Sino-American alliance has no raison d'etre, economically, politically, or in terms of mutual security interests. This does not preclude the development of a relationship sufficient to handle specific bilateral problems and to advance, within modest limits, such economic and cultural intercourse as is mutually beneficial. Such a relationship might also contribute significantly to the tackling of broader, multilateral issues like

---

[14] For a further elucidation of this theme, see the author's article, "The Sino-Soviet Dispute in Perspective," *The Annals of the American Academy of Political and Social Sciences*, January 1964, pp. 1-14.

those of peaceful coexistence and disarmament. An alliance, however, would be totally infeasible.[15]

Are the conditions more appropriate for a Sino-Japanese alliance? Throughout the twentieth century, such an alliance has been the dream of a number of Chinese and Japanese, and it continues to attract diverse individuals, both traditionalists and radicals. But, as we have seen, at present this type of development would have to involve a major Japanese accommodation to China. Some accommodation has been made by the new Tanaka government. But concessions of the dimensions that would provide the basis for an alliance could come about only after a veritable revolution in Japan, with the advent of a "left" government headed by the Japan Socialist party. Currently, such a turn of events is highly improbable. Indeed, although political instability may grow in Japan during this decade, even in the event of coalition government, the controlling elements would be non-Marxist. As we have noted, it is possible that the Japanese political tides will be strongly nationalist. Chinese versus Japanese nationalism thus cannot be ruled out as the central political competition in the Asian scene, despite the most recent developments.

A Chinese alliance with any of the major Pacific-Asian powers thus seems an unlikely prospect during the period ahead. Current

---

[15] For various important perspectives on the future of American-Chinese relations in addition to the works cited, see A. Doak Barnett, *A New U.S. Policy Toward China* (Washington, D.C.: The Brookings Institution, 1971); *Sino-American Relations, 1949-1971*, documented and introduced by Roderick Mac-Farquhar (New York: Praeger Publishers, Inc., 1971); and Richard Moorsteen and Morton Abramowitz, *Remaking China Policy* (Cambridge, Massachusetts: Harvard University Press, 1971).

Specifically on the Taiwan issue, for opposing views, see Lung-chu Chen and Harold D. Lasswell, *Formosa, China and the United States* (New York: St. Martin's Press, 1967); Jerome A. Cohen, Edward Friedman, Harold C. Hinton, and Allen S. Whiting, *Taiwan and American Policy—The Dilemma in U.S.-China Relations* (New York: Praeger Publishers, Inc., 1971); and Tang Tsou, ed., *China in Crisis*, vol. 2.

Two sets of hearings conducted in 1966 and 1970 by the Senate and House of Representatives remain useful: U.S. Congress, Senate Committee on Foreign Relations, *Hearings on U.S. Policy with Respect to Mainland China*, 89th Congress, 2d session, and House of Representatives, Subcommittee on Asian and Pacific Affairs of the Committee on Foreign Relations, *Hearings on United States-China Relations—A Strategy for the Future*, 91st Congress, 2d session.

Finally, for a work combining observations of China, 1971, with perspectives on Sino-American relations garnered from interviews with Chou En-lai and others, see the writings of *New York Times* newsmen, Tillman Durdin, James Reston and Seymour Topping, *Report from Red China* (New York: Quadrangle Books, Inc., 1971).

Chinese leaders have themselves recognized this fact. In recent conversations with foreigners, they have dwelt upon the importance of taking an independent, self-reliant stance in foreign affairs. Such talk, however, will not inhibit China from continuing or developing close ties with smaller states, some of them amounting to alliances. This will be particularly important to China's foreign policy in Asia as a part of its effort to achieve a favorable overall political-military position, or at least an equilibrium that will serve to check Soviet expansion. Such diverse states as Pakistan, Cambodia, and North Korea remain natural subjects for such ties.

United front. As a third alternative, let us consider a policy centering upon united front operations. Whereas alliance would place the emphasis upon an aggregation of power favoring China as defined in classical terms, a united front policy would put the stress upon an aggregation of power defined in modern revolutionary-political terms. The premium would thus be upon working closely with as many international revolutionary forces as possible, both those in and those out of power, Communists and non-Communists alike.

Clearly, this policy has a strong emotional appeal to men who consider themselves revolutionaries and who are in vigorous competition for leadership of the now-amorphous "revolutionary world." At certain times, moreover, the People's Republic of China has come close to making this its official policy. When Sukarno was in power in Indonesia, when Nkrumah was the leader in Ghana, and when men of similar type headed other Afro-Asian-Latin American countries, Peking made a major effort to identify with these "third world" forces, even to the extent of supporting Sukarno's organizational efforts to create a body that would rival the United Nations.

Current manifestations of this policy can be seen in China's sponsorship of the so-called Alliance of Indochinese People, and one of its key symbols, Prince Sihanouk. Nor is this the only example that could be cited. China continues its commitments to projects in Africa and the Middle East intended to bolster its united front position, notably the Tanzanian-Zambia railway construction project, and a host of more minor programs. Great interest has also been shown in such groups as the Black Panthers in the United States, with several invitations extended for visits to Peking, even after the Nixon trip.

In such policies, racism, specifically an anti-white bias, is to be discerned—although any Chinese pretension that racial equality with blacks or browns is widely accepted among their people is ironic indeed. The main reason for such policies, of course, is political—China's desire both to apply Communist doctrines in such a way as to benefit its national interests and to compete effectively with the Soviet Union for influence throughout the "revolutionary" non-Western world.

Undoubtedly, united front policies will continue as an element, possibly an important element, in Chinese foreign relations. But can they constitute the main stream? Perhaps they were more appealing when China was allowed to play only the revolutionary role on the international stage, when involvement in organizations like the United Nations and its supplementary units was not possible. In any case, the Chinese have already discovered that efforts to lead or influence the "third world," even the "revolutionary third world," produce multiple frustrations and can be extremely disappointing.

Given the divided nature of the international left at present, and given the much greater resources of the Soviet Union for united front efforts, the People's Republic has suffered repeated setbacks or failures, despite its best efforts. Thus, China's relations with Castro are now cool, primarily because only the Soviet Union can deliver what Castro must have. Similarly, in the Middle East, the Chinese in recent years have generally had to pick up the crumbs from beneath the Soviet table. In Asia, where the rivalry with the Soviet Union is most intense, uncertainties and disappointments have also been extensive. Fear of China has vied with desire for Chinese support, even among many Asian revolutionaries and especially among those whose countries border this giant.

Thus, it is by no means clear that the People's Republic will wield great influence upon the revolutionaries of the smaller states of East Asia merely by "good deeds." Force or the threat of force may be required, especially as long as the Soviet Union stands in the wings, and sometimes, indeed, at the front of the stage.

In sum, from Peking's point of view, the payoff from united front policies scarcely seems sufficient to make them the central element in Chinese foreign policy, particularly in an era when the People's Republic can deal as easily with a wide range of governments in power. By the same token, however, such policies are not likely to be abandoned totally, and on occasion they may be of great importance.

31

Pan-Asianism. Yet another possible alternative for the P.R.C. is Pan-Asianism. Such a policy also has strong appeal, especially if linked with a united front. ·Chinese leaders are fond of asserting that their relations with peoples like the North Koreans and North Vietnamese are those "of lips and teeth." They repeatedly guarantee that China will serve as "the secure revolutionary rear" for these small, peripheral states. Moreover, on occasion, Pan-Asianism has had broader implications. In the days when Nehru and Chou were both newly arrived at power, a great deal of rhetoric was spent on the need for Asians to determine the future of Asia and to cooperate in removing the West from Asia. More recently, Chinese leaders have indicated to *certain* Japanese, notably representatives of the Socialist and Kōmeitō parties, how vitally important close ties between China and Japan could be, if "progressives" of the two nations would unite.[16]

Once again, however, while Pan-Asianism may well be one ingredient in China's future foreign policies, it seems unlikely to become the dominant one. A Sino-Japanese alliance which would serve as the linchpin for such a policy appears remote, as we have suggested. A Sino-Indian alliance is even less likely. Yet unless one of these alliances materializes, Pan-Asianism cannot become the foundation of Chinese foreign policy.

Gaullism. Finally, let us explore the policy we have called Gaullism. If Gaullism is defined as a foreign policy putting a high premium upon nationalistic, independent positions coupled with a strong military posture, the People's Republic of China can be said to be pursuing a Gaullist policy now. In recent years, Chinese leaders have indicated disillusionment with alliances and wariness toward tightly knit multilateral involvement. Despite verbal assurances of support for "proletarian internationalism," moreover, a position of aloof independence and determined self-sufficiency accords both with China's classic political culture and its new nationalism. Self-sufficiency, it should be emphasized, requires extensive military power in the view of current Chinese leaders. They have made it unmistakably clear that they intend to spend whatever is necessary in order to achieve impressive strength in aircraft, submarines and all modern weaponry, nuclear weapons included.

---

[16] Chou's conversation with Japanese Socialist and Kōmeitō leaders have been carried in the organs of the two parties, *Shakai Shimpō* [The Socialist news] and *Kōmei Shimbun* [The Kōmei news].

Will Gaullism also be the Chinese foreign policy of the future? First, let us explore briefly the foreign policy goals which China is likely to pursue. Much of China's foreign policy in the next few years will undoubtedly be defensive in character, representing an effort to improve Chinese security. At the same time, as noted earlier, it will not always be easy to distinguish "defensive" and "offensive" actions. Almost certainly, the Chinese movement away from isolationism will continue, and a more intricate set of relations with both non-Communist and Communist states will develop. As in the foreign policy of any major state, paradoxes and contradictions will abound—especially in the juxtaposition of state-to-state and comrade-to-comrade relations.

Rhetorically, and via limited economic and military aid programs, China will remain committed to global revolution. Especially it will seek to serve as spokesman and champion of the "third world." At the same time, moreover, it will continue the effort to wrest from Moscow the ideological and political leadership of the international Communist movement.

In the allocation of both concerns and resources, however, China will be forced to give primary attention to Asia. Toward the small states of Asia, and particularly those on its border, China will continue the carrot and stick policies of the past. Those who exhibit "friendly" attitudes will be rewarded via recognition, aid and minimal interference in their internal affairs. Those considered "hostile" will be punished, with Peking supporting internal "liberation" movements and using other means of retaliation.

By these methods, and also by developing a credible nuclear deterrent as rapidly as possible, the Chinese will hope to thwart Soviet efforts to encircle China. The Soviet threat, of course, will be Peking's greatest concern because it involves every level of politics: domestic, border, and international. At the same time, however, China will seek to develop its own containment policy against Japan, seeking to confine Japan politically and militarily to its four main islands and to prevent any translation of Japanese economic power into political or military uses. Moreover, the P.R.C. will continue to push for the reduction of the American presence in Asia, especially the removal of close-in American military forces.[17]

---

[17] It should be noted, however, that Chou En-lai reportedly told two American congressional leaders, Hale Boggs (D., La.) and Gerald R. Ford (R., Mich.), recently that the People's Republic of China did not want the United States to

Taken together, these policies represent a mix of "defensive" and "offensive" responses. In seeking to bolster its security, China will be probing for, or actually asserting, hegemony throughout significant parts of Asia. In seeking to defeat the Russians politically and ideologically within the Communist and developing worlds, it will be giving voice to its own qualifications for leadership. And in attempting to contain Japan and India, China will be seeking a greater role in Asia for itself, protestations to the contrary notwithstanding.

In general, these policies point to the continuance of Gaullism as the central core of Chinese foreign policy, but a Gaullism modified by special ties with secondary states and by a liberal admixture of united front and Pan-Asian policies. China will continue to stand apart from the other major Pacific-Asian states, but not equidistant from each of them. Varying degrees of competition-cooperation and of friendliness-normalcy-hostility will mark such relationships.

Potentially at least, China's relations with the Soviet Union could be characterized by considerable swings of the pendulum, influenced by factors of accident on the international scene and internal political developments within both societies. At this point, the odds favor a continuance of strongly hostile, relatively minimal relations. It is in this relationship, however, that the most dramatic changes could conceivably take place. Relations with India are almost certain to remain strained, with the Himalayan region representing both a barrier and a source of tension. Sino-Japanese relations could well become more important to China, particularly in the economic sphere. Emotional factors in Japan's relations with its Chinese "half-brothers" are also complex, some of them favoring closer ties. Still, the massive differences in the institutions and the values of these two societies would seem to preclude the development of intimate relations. Competition far more than cooperation is likely to dominate Sino-Japanese relations. Finally, relations with the United States can be convenient for China, and on occasion perhaps highly significant. But in-depth, intimate bilateral relations traversing the economic, political and cultural fields do not seem remotely possible. The United States and China are societies distant from each other in almost every conceivable sense, and although this can serve to preclude conflict, it will also rule out any sense of close identity.

leave Asia at this point, since such a departure might lend weight to a greater Soviet presence or renewed Japanese militarism.

Thus, China appears destined to have contact with all major states in the era ahead, but truly intimate relations with none. The impact of this upon regional relations is explored in chapter 4.

India: Regional or International Power?

It remains to discuss briefly the foreign policy alternatives of India and Indonesia, two Asian states that are significant in terms of population, area, and resources.

The Ingredients of Power. Is it appropriate to consider India a major power? This question brings to mind some of the same factors that must be considered when a similar question is posed regarding China. Both of these societies knew military power, sometimes very great power, in the course of their long histories. Generally speaking, however, such power was secondary to other concerns; the predominate tendency of each society was to look inward rather than outward in the course of its development, despite the fact that both were subject to successive waves of foreign invaders. They shared a deep sense of self-sufficiency, cultural separateness, and an only occasional interest in involvement in the outside world.

There are also some highly important differences between China and India, ranging from the geographic to the political and psychological. South Asia is essentially peripheral to the Eurasian continent, with the Himalaya Mountains constituting a major land barrier. Despite the historic invasions over that barrier (and the Chinese intrusion of 1962), India is not an integral part of the region to the north. In culture also, it has been distinct both from the West and from the Sinic societies of Northeast Asia. Thus, political separatism comes easily, alliance only with great difficulty. Equally important, India is the first of the major Pacific-Asian societies considered here that possesses a very recent colonial legacy. Independence was achieved only in 1947. That independence, moreover, came amidst great trauma and bloodshed, involving not the colonial power, Great Britain, but rather fratricidal struggle among groups of different religious-cultural heritages. Both colonialism and the events surrounding independence have naturally colored Indian views of the world. They have also shaped Indian priorities in foreign and domestic policies.

The Nehru Legacy. Nevertheless, in the first critical years after British rule ended, those views and priorities were seen through the perceptions and biases of a single man, Jawaharlal Nehru. Nehru—intellectual, Fabian Socialist, product of the Indian elite and Cambridge—had a strong animus against the West, and particularly the United States. His foreign policy centered upon two goals, neutralism and Pan-Asianism.

Neutralism reflected both ideological and pragmatic considerations. Nehru viewed India as standing apart from both the Communist bloc and the West, headed by the United States. In a bipolar world, India would serve to rally a third group, the newly emerging states of the non-West. In this fashion, a separate force would be created, capable of exercising leverage upon the major power blocs. India itself would be the principal leader of this third force, but its influence would take the form not of military power but of moral and political authority. Thus, Indian foreign policy would involve minimal risks and commitments. With domestic issues both pressing and extremely complex, the first priorities had to go to the home front. Nation-building and economic development would consume Indian energies—and resources—for the foreseeable future. Foreign policy had to support rather than sap domestic development.

Pan-Asianism was a second pillar of Indian foreign policy in the early Nehru era, reflecting Nehru's anti-West sentiments. The Indian prime minister envisaged a special relation or understanding between the two massive Asian societies, India and China, that would enable a settlement of Asian problems without Western involvement. He regarded the ideological, political and cultural differences between the two states of less moment than the fact that both had shared a common legacy in relations with the West and that both were Asian states dedicated to ending Western influence in that region of the world. And he believed that in the event of Indian-Chinese agreement and leadership, the other Asian states would follow them.

There was a mixture of arrogance and unreality in Nehru's policies, along with awareness of India's needs and capacities. In the beginning, these policies appeared to be highly successful. Rapport with China was established (at a certain cost on an issue like Tibet); India's, and more particularly, Nehru's, international prestige soared, enabling influence to be exercised in the councils of the Afro-Asian world; and peaceful coexistence appeared on the verge of becoming an operative principle in relations among the major Asian states.

At the close of his career, however, Nehru's foreign policy was in tatters. Pan-Asianism proved to be a chimera. By the end of the 1950s, India and China were locked in a bitter dispute centering upon boundary issues but reflecting broader problems. Even before the 1962 war in which India suffered a resounding defeat, its prestige had sunk to a low point throughout the world. In the early Nehru era, India had been the most prestigious state in Asia, with wide-ranging relations throughout the Afro-Asian region, whereas China had been largely isolated and heavily dependent upon the Soviet Union. A decade later, the situation was almost precisely the reverse. China was cutting a wide swath in the non-West, exercising leadership in such groups as the Afro-Asian Solidarity Conference and even establishing its own aid programs. India, on the other hand, placed on the defensive by events, was turning increasingly to the Soviet Union for political and military aid.[18]

India's hope was to maintain relatively balanced relations with the two superpowers, obtaining economic and military assistance from both the United States and the U.S.S.R. From the outset, however, this hope ran into difficulties. While the United States was prepared to aid India economically and provide military assistance against the China threat, it had treaty obligations to Pakistan, both via the Southeast Asia Treaty Organization (SEATO) and the Central Treaty Organization (CENTO). Moreover, the United States believed that peace on the South Asian subcontinent required a military balance between the two major states of the region, Pakistan and India.

On such issues as Kashmir, India proved to be absolutely intransigent, and two conflicts with Pakistan ensued. Gradually, a rough political-military equilibrium appeared to develop, with Pakistan acquiring an increasingly close relationship with China, India drawing ever nearer

---

[18] For recent studies on Indian foreign policy, see Leo E. Rose, "India," in *Asia and the International System*, pp. 61-92; William J. Barnds, *India, Pakistan and the Great Powers* (New York: Praeger Publishers, Inc., 1972); and Shelton L. Williams, *The United States, India and the Bomb* (Baltimore: Johns Hopkins Press, 1969).

Older works still having great utility, and offering differing perspectives include W. Norman Brown, *The United States and India and Pakistan* (Cambridge, Massachusetts: Harvard University Press, 1963); and Selig S. Harrison, ed., *India and the United States* (New York: The Macmillan Co., 1961); and for an emphasis upon Sino-Indian relations, K. M. Panikkar, *In Two Chinas: Memoirs of a Diplomat* (London: G. Allen & Unwin, 1955); John Rowland, *A History of Sino-Indian Relations—Hostile Coexistence* (Princeton, New Jersey: Van Nostrand-Reinhold Co., 1967); and Wayne A. Wilcox, *India, Pakistan and the Rise of China* (New York: Walker and Co., 1964).

to the Soviet Union, and the United States taking a neutral stance. In 1971, however, this equilibrium was broken. In its intervention into Pakistani territory on behalf of the secessionist Bangladesh movement, India scored a smashing military victory, with full Russian political support. Not only was Pakistan reduced to half its former self and removed from any chance of equaling Indian power, but China was also adversely affected, since despite its violent rhetoric, it had been totally unable to influence the outcome. Moreover, Indian-American relations sank to a new low, with the United States highly critical of Indian military actions and pursuing a policy "tilted" against New Delhi. In the course of this crisis, moreover, India finally abandoned its nonalignment policy, despite vigorous denials, and entered into an alliance with the Soviet Union via a "friendship pact."

Contemporary India and Foreign Policy Alternatives. Thus, today, India is aligned and, in effect, serves as part of the Soviet Union's containment policy against the People's Republic of China. India is also dominant on the subcontinent, with no formidable competitor in sight, although in the long run its relations with the smaller states of the region, including Bangladesh, may produce serious problems that affect both domestic and foreign policies. Meanwhile, however, Indian spirits have been greatly lifted by the major military victory over Pakistan, particularly since points were thereby scored against both China and the United States. Nationalism has reached its highest point and the Indian military, once ridiculed, has acquired a new prestige.

Under these conditions, what are the future alternatives for Indian foreign policy? A return to the old Nehruian policy of nonalignment coupled with pacifism and Pan-Asianism seems so unlikely as to be ruled out as a feasible alternative. Basically, India faces two separate, yet interrelated, issues. Shall the movement toward alliance with the Soviet Union be maintained and advanced; or shall some effort be made to return to relatively balanced relations with the two superpowers, and hence, to some degree of nonalignment? Secondly, shall India continue to subordinate foreign policy generally to domestic commitments, retaining the position of regional dominance now acquired but eschewing involvement outside the subcontinent; or shall it take a more active role in regions such as Southeast Asia and possibly expand ties with Japan also?

Alliance. From the perspective of India's current leaders, a strong case can be made for a policy of continued alliance with the U.S.S.R. Until recently at least, Soviet credibility in Asia was at an all-time high. The Russians had demonstrated that they possessed power and the will to use it. The United States, on the other hand, is widely believed in India to be withdrawing from Asia and hence American commitments, particularly those involving security, are deemed of dubious value, even if they could be obtained—which is highly doubtful. In recent months, Soviet problems with Egypt and the uncertain character of Soviet commitments to North Vietnam have raised doubts in certain quarters in India concerning Russian credibility. As long as relations with China remain strained and potentially dangerous, however, ties with Russia represent the best form of protection. Moreover, up to date, the Soviet alliance has proven beneficial to Mrs. Gandhi and the left Congress party on the home front. It has further underwritten the working arrangement with the Communist party of India (CPI), the Moscow-oriented "right wing Communist party." This arrangement in turn has served to deepen the divisions within Indian Communist ranks and has provided Mrs. Gandhi and her party with maximum power and leverage —although recently, problems, some of them potentially serious, have surfaced between the left Congress and the CPI.

In any case, over the long run this alliance may create serious new problems for India, both at home and abroad. Will not a divided Indian left now be more likely to be involved in every twist and turn in international Communist relations, particularly in Sino-Soviet relations? Does not the alliance make less likely any normalization of relations with China and strengthen the probability of various forms of Chinese retaliation, notably with respect to border areas, tribal peoples, and elements within the Indian political scene itself? Are not the risks for Indian involvement in international controversies now increased, and rapport with those comrades of yesteryear, the so-called nonaligned bloc, made more difficult—as the recent Georgetown Conference of Non-Aligned Nations illustrated? Finally, can India under Soviet alliance escape the unhappy fate of Egypt, where excessive Soviet influence and deep policy differences finally burst into the open?

Not all officials in the Indian government, and not even all anti-American elements, are oblivious to these possibilities. Indeed, some review of policy is taking place. It is not surprising that Prime Minister Gandhi vigorously denies that India has departed from its policies of nonalignment and insists that the 1971 friendship pact and other ties with the U.S.S.R. do not constitute an alliance. She is aware of an additional problem, namely, the deep unhappiness of certain other South Asian states such as Ceylon and Nepal with the new Indian policies. If the Soviet Union moves into the Indian Ocean, with either the support or tolerance of India, and establishes a commanding presence throughout this region, will this not bring added complications to those smaller states attempting to retain nonalignment as a central principle?

Regionalism versus broader commitments. Meanwhile, India must decide whether it desires to play a larger role in the world, particularly in Asia. The struggle for supremacy in South Asia now appears to have been won decisively, although the problems created by Bangladesh seem likely to prove serious at some point. Does India have sufficient interest in Southeast Asia to make additional commitments there?

Recurrently, the Indians have shown concern over the security of Burma, and its internal developments. This is understandable. Burma has lengthy borders—some of them traversing wild terrain—with one of India's most troublesome regions, the Northeast Territories. Peopled by Naga and other tribal groups, these border areas provide a temptation to China, because intervention via ethnic politics can be undertaken at relatively low cost. The Ne Win government has also felt the impact of Chinese intervention periodically, notably through China's aid to the White Flag Burmese Communists. The possibility always exists, therefore, of an Indian-Burmese de facto alliance, or at a minimum close security ties, possibly linked into a Soviet aid program directed toward both states. Overtures in this direction have periodically been made, but Burma remains exceedingly cautious of any involvement with India for understandable reasons. Under the British, Burma was for a time governed as a part of the Indian administration. Anti-Indian sentiment remains strong at the grass roots levels of Burmese society. Moreover, the reaction of China to any Indian-Burmese alignment would be highly adverse—and, as we have seen, China has leverage here via the White Flag Burmese Communists.

India's recent decision to grant full diplomatic recognition to the Democratic Republic of Vietnam (North Vietnam) signals Mrs. Gandhi's deep hostility to Washington. It may also be taken as an effort to establish ties with another small state proclaiming itself Communist but believed to be interested in maintaining its independence from China.

40

Thus, at this point, India's recent projections into Southeast Asia seem closely connected to its alliance with the Soviet Union, representing efforts to align with small "socialist" states currently neutral or hostile to the United States but anxious to avoid excessive Chinese influence. In this sense, India is playing a role in the Soviet-directed effort to contain China, a fact which Peking clearly perceives.

There is little evidence, however, to suggest that India intends to expand its role in Asia greatly. Even in Southeast Asia, although long advocating "neutralization" as the most appropriate stance for the region, India has been too weak and too unconcerned to play an influential part in directing concrete efforts toward that end. Indeed, while intensely critical of American policies there, India has been prepared to benefit from them, conscious that the U.S. presence makes it less necessary for India to undertake any positive involvement in a region of considerable importance to its security and economic interests. Meanwhile, Indian relations with Japan might increase substantially during the next decade, but it is very doubtful whether such relations will go far beyond the economic realm. Even in this respect, if current trends toward emphasizing the public sector and inhibiting the private sector continue in India, Japanese-Indian economic ties may be less than some have anticipated, particularly if problems in economic planning and development continue at their present levels.

By the end of the 1970s, however, it is possible that India will take a step that would greatly alter its position in Asia, namely, the acquisition of nuclear weapons. Like the Japanese, the Indians intend to keep their nuclear options open, watching developments in East Asia and in the world. Thus, while a greatly expanded set of foreign commitments is not in prospect now, it cannot be ruled out for the middle- and longer-range future. In terms of active, direct participation, India will have a limited influence upon Asia outside the subcontinent in the years immediately ahead. Nevertheless, alliance with the Soviet Union—granted that this alliance allows flexibility—casts India in a new role. Perforce, India is now an important element in the complex balance of power currently coming into being in the area as a whole. It is clearly a partner—though a junior, partly reluctant partner—in the Soviet effort to contain China at this point. As long as that alliance is maintained, it will have an increasing influence upon both Indian domestic and foreign policies, providing a certain momentum for greater involvement abroad.

The deep ambivalence characterizing India's approach to international relations is likely to continue, however. India will cultivate power and, at the same time, will reject any analysis that accords power a central role in the international political scene. Concurrently, it will seek self-sufficiency and concentrate upon its massive internal problems while also looking for ways to increase its authority in the broader community of Asia.

Indonesia: Southeast Asia's Primary Society

Indonesia, as the most important nation in Southeast Asia, has many of the ingredients of power. The Indonesians have fashioned a nation stretching over 3,000 miles in a vast island chain and encompassing a population of 125 million that is still expanding. The nation displays great diversity, possessing not one, but several high cultures, a testimony to its people's capacities. It is a country of abundant resources, including raw materials and energy sources that will be the objective of intensive competition among the developed and developing nations in the decades immediately ahead.

The Sukarno Era. In its recent past, moreover, Indonesia has shown how power can be misused. President Sukarno camouflaged domestic failures with foreign adventurism. With Indonesia wallowing in economic chaos and having abandoned parliamentarism in favor of "guided democracy," Sukarno plunged his nation into a series of foreign escapades. In their most expanded form, Sukarno's policies represented nothing less than an effort to challenge the existing world order. In addition to extensive efforts on behalf of such groups as the Afro-Asian Solidarity Conference, Sukarno, in company with Peking, sought to establish a rival organization to the United Nations. Having withdrawn Indonesia from the U.N., he was in the course of constructing an edifice in Djakarta to house an association of Newly Emerging States at the time of his overthrow. Meanwhile, he had undertaken a "confrontation" with Malaysia, sending guerrilla forces against the new government which he labelled a tool of British imperialism. Indeed, Sukarno's united front policies aligned Indonesia increasingly with China, North Korea and North Vietnam, and constituted a menacing pincer movement against the non-Communist states of Southeast Asia.

42

In the end, however, these policies proved counterproductive. Gradually, Indonesia became a pariah in the region, with most other Southeast Asian states regarding it with a mixture of concern and contempt. The grandiose schemes for Afro-Asian-Latin American unity and for a counterpart organization to the United Nations fell apart, rendering the Indonesian president the object of increasing ridicule. More importantly, perhaps, his policies contributed significantly to the American decision to retain a presence in Southeast Asia, and to support those with whom it had treaty obligations against Indonesian threats or united front pincer movements. It was the American view that unless the policies of confrontation and violence against legally established governments in this region ceased, the hope for any overall political-military equilibrium in Asia would be lost and the prospects for a larger war made much greater.

By the mid-1960s, Sukarno's foreign policies were in as much difficulty as his domestic policies, a factor possibly accounting for the timing of the abortive leftist coup—although the President's uncertain health seems to have been the principal consideration. The details of the attempted coup are still in dispute, but there seems little doubt that the primary target was the army leadership, with the key coup leaders being drawn from Communist and "leftist" ranks. Apparently the hope was to settle Sukarno's succession and liquidate key anti-Communist elements before the leader died. When the coup failed, events developed in a reverse fashion. Hundreds of thousands of Communists (and others) were killed or imprisoned. Sukarno himself ultimately became a well-guarded prisoner in one of his palaces. A new era had commenced.

The Alternatives for Indonesian Foreign Policy. The Indonesian events of 1965-66 illustrate the hazards of predicting and projecting the foreign policies of any state subject to radical fluctuations in its domestic politics. Similarly dramatic developments could occur, as has already been noted, in some of the other nations discussed in this study. Even if such changes were to take place within the established system, so to speak, they could be extremely important.

The new military government of Indonesia headed by General Suharto, to be sure, has not abandoned the past completely. Nonalignment continues to be voiced as an expression of the government's determination to remain aloof from major power conflicts. The present hope is to use as many major nations as possible for what is now regarded as the

43

primary objective, that of economic development. Once again, priorities have been reordered, as Indonesia seeks to make up for the time so tragically lost in the Sukarno era. Current policies of nonalignment, however, have a decided tilt toward non-Communist nations and causes. The Indonesian Communist movement, together with the old actions and attitudes of Peking toward Indonesia, evoke bitter memories. Many of the men now in power were marked for Communist bullets, a fact not likely to be forgotten.

Indonesia-first. Thus, Indonesia possesses relatively few foreign policy alternatives at present. For the foreseeable future, foreign policy will be used as a handmaiden to internal development. Inevitably, issues of independence, involving the capacity and will to control one's own resources, will emerge as Indonesia calls upon external sources for major assistance. The present leaders believe there is safety in numbers and hence solicit involvement from a number of states. They are concerned about the possible overweening influence of Japan, however, the nation most likely to predominate in Indonesian economic development.

Taking advantage of the Sino-Soviet cleavage, Indonesia has achieved some degree of normalized relations with the Soviet Union, its anti-Communist policies notwithstanding. An olive branch is even timidly extended to China, despite the fact that a few surviving prominent Indonesian Communists now reside permanently in Peking. And the ties previously established with North Korea and North Vietnam have not been broken, although the representatives of these states maintain a very low posture. Such policies indicate a degree of flexibility in Indonesian foreign policy suited to a nation that has little interest currently in ideological politics, continues to harbor some suspicions of all foreigners, and covets an Indonesia-first policy concentrating upon the domestic front.[19]

Regionalism. Nonetheless, one important issue cannot be avoided. To what extent should Indonesia participate in, and seek to lead a drive toward, Southeast Asian regionalism? Do the nations of this area hold a sufficient number of common economic, political and security concerns to make regionalism practicable, and how should it be advanced? Once again, we are faced with a problem which evokes both

---

[19] For an excellent brief summary of recent trends in Indonesian foreign policy, see Franklin Weinstein, "Indonesia," in *Asia and the International Order,* pp. 116-145.

rational and emotional responses, not always in concert with each other. In every respect—culturally, economically, politically, and in terms of its security—Indonesia is inextricably connected with mainland Southeast Asia, especially with Malaysia. The failure to recognize this central fact is the fatal weakness of any island *cordon sanitaire* strategy, any theory based on the notion that a defense line could rest upon the island chain off mainland Asia. Indonesia can never avoid being deeply influenced by developments on the Malay peninsula or in Borneo, an island which the Indonesians share with Malaysia. In turn, this gives Indonesia a strong interest in the trends governing Thailand and the states of Indochina.

It is not surprising, therefore, that whether under Sukarno or Suharto, and irrespective of the methods used and the goals sought, Indonesia should continue to exhibit an abiding interest in helping to bring Southeast Asia together through a variety of regional undertakings. As the largest and most powerful nation of the region, moreover, Indonesia naturally expects to play a leading role in all such endeavors. With a population nearly equaling that of the rest of Southeast Asia combined and with an army of some 400,000, it is a logical leader.

At the same time, the obstacles confronting an effective Southeast Asian regionalism are impressive, as are the risks to any nation undertaking its sponsorship. The long history of animosities among the peoples of this area need not be recounted here. Those animosities have rested upon a wide range of differences, with ethnic-cultural diversities serving as their foundation. Conflicts between hill and valley peoples, between Buddhists, Christians and the followers of Islam, and between Chinese and Malays have been endemic. In modern times, moreover, the intervention of major powers from outside the region has added further complications.

Thus, while regional cooperation and the development of institutions to further it constitute a critical need, progress is likely to be slow and uneven. Major power agreement on neutralization for some or all of the region, coupled with the establishment of a workable system of peaceful coexistence to free the region of the constant threat of externally aided "civil wars," would greatly abet Southeast Asian regionalism. The regional route, however, even with those advantages, will remain rocky and uncertain.

3

The U.S. and the U.S.S.R. in Asia

The Soviet Union: An Expanding Force

The average Russian must contend today with two images of Asia. As a good Marxist-Leninist, he is taught that class, not race or culture, plays the determining role in building solidarity and that he has proletarian status in common with millions of his Asian brethren. More than this, by virtue of his state's superior power and of the fact that the first Communist revolution took place there, he has a special responsibility to serve as model and, if need be, as savior of later, less powerful fraternal comrades—be they East Europeans or Asians. To be sure, interest in and commitment to such tasks have faded as second and third generation revolutionaries have emerged and as the Russian people have become increasingly preoccupied with the challenges of internal development.

Meanwhile, an older image stubbornly retains its vitality in the Russian mind, the image of limitless Asian hordes sweeping over the vast plains toward the heart of the motherland. This is an image at once dark, terrifying and impregnated with strong racial feelings. The advent of Communist rule, moreover, has done little to remove it. On the contrary, under the Communists, Russia has come into ever greater contact, both physically and politically, with the seemingly endless world of Asia. The empire has expanded under the commissars as it did under the czars, moving the Russians to the very edge of the major societies of Eastern Asia. Far from increasing their feelings of security, this has caused apprehension to mount.

47

The Evolution of Soviet Policy in Asia. In the more than 50 years since the Bolshevik Revolution, four broad phases of Soviet interaction with East Asia can be discerned. At the outset, Soviet foreign policy catered to two overarching objectives: first, to defend the Communist regime against those who would overthrow it from within and without and, second, to protect the new Russia as a vanguard of global revolution. Asia could be utilized for both of those purposes. By making common cause with the diverse nationalist movements of Asia, the Russian Communist leaders hoped to exploit a revolutionary opportunity of enormous potential. Asia could be turned against the West and that protégé of the West, Japan. And by striking hard against their primary opponents in this fashion, the Union of Soviet Socialist Republics would achieve defense and revolution simultaneously.

Thus, for a decade after 1917, Bolshevik leaders expended both treasure and personnel in lavish amounts upon Asia, and particularly upon China. Intensive involvement, however, ended in failure and disillusionment. "Who lost China?" was a question asked in Moscow two decades before it was raised in Washington. In the second stage, therefore, Soviet leaders turned their attention back to Europe. Once again, the prime importance of Europe to Russian security was brought home through the rise of Hitler. The vanquished of World War I were reemerging, and Russia was one of the targets.

The hope of using Asia to bolster Soviet security was resurrected, but, as in the earlier era, Asia generally proved to be a weak reed. Fervently, via the Comintern, Moscow called for a union of all revolutionaries and "patriotic bourgeois" forces to fight fascism. The Chinese Communists, among others, responded. But these were perilous times for the Soviet Union. The Russians came very close to fighting a war with Germany and Japan simultaneously, and with minimal international support. The threat of a two-front war on the Eurasian continent, indeed, is one that no Russian leader is likely to overlook, given the experiences of this century.

Fortunately for the Russians, however, Japan elected to turn southward, thereby bringing the United States into the war. With this event, the Asian threat was contained and the Soviet leaders could concentrate on the awesome task of meeting German armies with their recently purged Russian military forces. Up to mid-1945, they contented themselves with plans for a future Asian role, plans broadly accepted

48

by their Western allies at Yalta in exchange for a Soviet pledge to enter the Asian war at a suitable time.

Thus, the stage was set for a third phase of Soviet-Asian relations in the years immediately following World War II. Rapidly, as Soviet-American relations deteriorated, the Russians divided Asia, together with other critical areas of the world, into two categories, "friendly" and "hostile." Bipolarism here as elsewhere was the ruling principle, with neutralism given short shrift. Against "hostile" Asia, namely, those portions of Asia aligned with the United States or other non-Communist states, the Russians were prepared to encourage "liberation" wars and other disruptive acts. Once again, Asia was to be used as a revolutionary staging ground, as a part of a broader campaign against the West, and particularly the United States. Now, however, the objectives could scarcely be defined as defensive. The socialist stage of the revolution was emerging, it was proclaimed, and capitalism was in its death throes.

Nevertheless, while Moscow gave full moral support and considerable material aid to "friendly" Asia in this era, circumstances dictated that its first priorities were to bind the deep wounds of the Soviet Union itself and to establish the Soviet presence firmly in Europe. In comparison, Asia was of strictly secondary importance. Moreover, confident of its own leadership and of the solidarity of the Communist bloc, the U.S.S.R. accepted a division of labor following the Communist victory in China. While Moscow was overseeing the emergence of communism in Europe, the Chinese would assume responsibility for the East Asian theater.

To be sure, this agreement was never absolute, and it probably was not defined in clear-cut terms. For example, throughout the Stalinist era, the Soviet Union continued to play the primary role in North Korea. Yet it was the Chinese who fought and died there when Communist miscalculation produced a war with the United States. Moreover, Peking's growing influence—material as well as ideological—was soon revealed in some Communist parties, such as those of Japan, Vietnam and Indonesia.

With the advent of the Sino-Soviet dispute, however, a fourth stage of Soviet relations with Asia was entered. Bipolarism in every sense was now inadequate. Neither the Communist nor the non-Communist states could be considered a bloc. On the contrary, the primary threat came from the People's Republic of China, not because of China's superior military power, but because the New China confronted the U.S.S.R. so intensely and so completely as to jeopardize the entire Soviet system. Peking's assertion that Khrushchev and his successors have departed from true Marxism-Leninism and have been attempting to restore capitalism in Russia strikes at the very legitimacy of the government, and at party-citizen relations. Suddenly, the historic weapons of the Russians in foreign policy, namely, people-to-people and comrade-to-comrade relations, are being turned against them in a profoundly subversive manner by others vying for the Marxist-Leninist mantle. For more than a decade at this point, Moscow and Peking have perforce been deeply and inextricably involved in each other's internal affairs. Nothing could be better calculated than this to render their mutual relations bitter in the extreme.

Nor is this all. At every point, the leaders of the People's Republic of China challenge the Soviet right to lead or even speak on behalf of the international revolutionary movement. Thus, the historic motherland of all proletarian fighters must now fight to hold a vanguard position. Indeed, nationalism—formerly a weapon most valuable to Soviet leaders in their utilization of the forces of the non-Western world—is currently turned against them, with charges of "great nation chauvinism" and "social imperialism" ringing through the air, directed at Moscow. In this fashion, "the revolutionary world," now many worlds and bitterly divided, has ceased to be an asset to the Soviet Union, particularly in Asia.

Even in terms of classical power, China currently represents a serious problem to the Soviet Union. Another continental-mass society, China possesses both manpower and territory in abundance, and it lies alongside the sparsely populated regions of Soviet Asia. The Chinese, moreover, have displayed a sense of power in all its forms and uses as shrewd as any opponent that Russia has faced in recent times. Even before the dispute with Moscow developed, China signaled its intent to obtain nuclear weapons. Indeed, that became one of the immediate causes for the cleavage. How could the U.S.S.R. rest easily when its giant neighbor insisted upon adding nuclear arms to its conventional military capability?

With estrangement came an accelerated Chinese drive to acquire allies or special ties to offset Soviet influence and power. Some of these efforts—notably those involving Albania, Rumania and Yugoslavia—reached deeply into the Soviet sphere of influence, violating Russia's outer defenses. Others were calculated to create additional Soviet costs

50

or worries, for example, with respect to Pakistan, Indochina, and not least of all, the United States.

Foreign Policy Alternatives for the Soviet Union. It is against this background that we should survey the meaningful Soviet foreign policy alternatives as they relate to Asia.[20]

A minimal foreign policy. Let us look first at the possibilities for a minimal policy, one envisaging a return to an inward-looking stance, involving some withdrawal and a larger quotient of isolationism. As in the case of China (and the United States), the Soviet Union possesses a cultural heritage that lends itself to such a policy. Another continental-mass society, Russia too has had a lengthy history of self-sufficiency, inwardness, and xenophobia. Isolation comes naturally to such a society. In modern times, moreover, Communist leaders enforced aloofness, wary of the impact which extensive foreign contacts might have upon the Russian people and anxious to avoid comparisons in a period when heavy sacrifices were being demanded on behalf of economic growth. In certain critical respects, therefore, Communist policies have reinforced the isolationist proclivities of Russia's historical political culture.

Paradoxically, however, the Soviet Union is the only major power that is currently expanding its commitments. In recent years, the U.S.S.R. has become a global rather than a regional power, taking on vast new responsibilities throughout the world. The intriguing question is whether these extensive commitments will produce a crisis of priorities similar to that recently witnessed in the United States. The Soviet consumer still has a huge list of unsatisfied desires. The Soviet economy continues to demonstrate weaknesses almost as impressive as its strengths. Will the Russian people, or perhaps more importantly portions of the Soviet elite, express displeasure at the growing number of foreign commitments using up Russian goods and services while domes-

---

[20] For insightful studies of Soviet foreign policy, see George F. Kennan, *Russia and the West Under Lenin and Stalin* (Boston: Little, Brown & Co., 1961); Charles B. McLane, *Soviet Strategies in Southeast Asia—An Exploration of Eastern Policy Under Lenin and Stalin* (Princeton, New Jersey: Princeton University Press, 1966); Marshall D. Shulman, *Stalin's Foreign Policy Reappraised* (Cambridge, Massachusetts: Harvard University Press, 1963), and *Beyond the Cold War* (New Haven, Connecticut: Yale University Press, 1966); and Adam B. Ulam, *Expansion and Coexistence: The History of Soviet Foreign Policy, 1917-1967* (New York: Praeger Publishers, Inc., 1968).

tic living standards remain low? Moreover, will recent crises, such as that involving Egypt, increase this likelihood?

The case against a minimal Soviet foreign policy, however, is exceedingly powerful, Russian political culture and contemporary public opinion notwithstanding. Communist ideology itself projects Soviet policy outward, providing the moral and political justification for broad international commitments. More importantly, however, Soviet leaders have greatly expanded their definition of security requirements. Not since World War II have the Russian leaders conceived of national defense in terms of Soviet border maintenance. Now, Russian security lines stretch from Central Europe in the West to the network of alliances in Asia through which the leadership hopes to guarantee its eastern defenses. Automatically, this involves the Soviet Union deeply and permanently in the international relations of both Europe and Asia.

Meanwhile, far-reaching new commitments in the Middle East and in certain areas of Africa and Latin America (Cuba) have now acquired a history and rationale of their own, notwithstanding recurrent setbacks. Any unilateral retreat from these commitments would be regarded as gravely injurious either to Soviet security or to Soviet prestige. Whether defended as part of the global strategy of a nation locked in competition with the United States, as policies necessary to ensure access to vital raw materials, or as the leadership posture required of the world's foremost Communist society, current regional commitments represent a distillation of the trials and errors of nearly three decades of active internationalism. They will be periodically adjusted as circumstances dictate, but they will not be abandoned lightly.

Moreover, there is no indication that Soviet public opinion, even if it were inclined toward a major retrenchment program, could prevail in the near future, given the nature of the Soviet system. On the contrary, recent policies, on balance, have probably heightened the power of the Soviet military, thereby providing new impetus toward an expansionist program.

United front. Is the reestablishment of a unified Communist bloc, once again under Soviet direction, a feasible goal—a possible second alternative for Soviet foreign policy? Unquestionably, Russian leaders must long for the era when Moscow was the ultimate authority in the Communist world, manipulating such instrumentalities as the Comintern and Cominform in its efforts to separate the orthodox from the hereti-

52

cal and to define as correct internationalism that which was deemed essential to Russian national interests. In some respects, moreover, the legacy of that era remains strong. In East Europe particularly, the Soviet Union has indicated in unmistakable terms that there is a line of permissible domestic and foreign policy beyond which no "socialist" nation may step. Here, and in Mongolia, the Russians show every indication of fighting if necessary to preserve their sphere of influence, thereby acknowledging that heavy involvement in the internal affairs of a number of its client states will continue.

Not even the most optimistic Russian leader, however, would assert that the reunification of the Communist world in a pattern similar to that which prevailed in earlier times can be accomplished. The task, indeed, is to prevent further slippage. Whether that requires tougher policies, or more flexible and subtle ones, will undoubtedly continue to be a matter of fierce internal debate. Meanwhile, however, the Russians are gradually discovering that some of their most important allies and critical relationships are to be found outside the Communist orbit. This fact makes exclusive reliance upon internationalism via Communist ties less attractive, quite apart from its infeasibility.

Increasingly, indeed, the Soviet Union has found it advantageous to interact positively with a wide range of governments, some of them very harshly disposed toward their domestic Communists. And it pursues these policies while, at the same time, utilizing every means short of war to attack certain states and parties calling themselves Communist but seen as a threat to Soviet interests. Thus, Moscow appears to find it neither possible nor desirable to reestablish a discrete, unified Communist bloc as the primary instrument of Soviet foreign policy.

Multilateralism. A third alternative for the U.S.S.R. might be the acceptance of a loosely knit multilateral system involving the sharing of responsibilities among a number of states. In part, such a system would offer a substitution for unilateral or bilateral pledges and guarantees. It would be in line with the widely heralded movement from bipolarism toward multipolarism.

How would such a policy have practical application in Asia? One example might be a multi-power guarantee of the "peaceful settlement" of the Korean unification issue, or "noninterference" in the internal affairs of the two Korean states. Such agreements would presumably be substituted for the current bilateral security treaties upon which both

53

South and North Korea rely. A similar substitution might be effected in the case of Japan, with multi-power guarantees taking the place of the U.S.-Japan Mutual Security Treaty. Loosely knit multilateralism may well be acceptable to the Soviet Union in those instances where it weakens opposing forces, or reduces Soviet responsibilities without any corresponding reduction in Soviet security or interests. Thus, it is very possible that Russia would welcome multilateral guarantees involving Japan or the Korean peninsula. Multilateral agreements relating to European security might also stir a genuine Soviet interest. After their achievement, NATO could be disbanded and the United States removed from the area. By virtue of geography, the Soviet Union would remain.

It is most difficult, however, to envisage Soviet acceptance of multilateralism as the cornerstone of Russian foreign policy. The Soviet leadership is not prepared to place its ultimate reliance upon multilateralism in any form in those areas, such as East Europe and Mongolia, where it considers Soviet interests to be preeminent and vital. Nor do its reservations stop with these core regions of concern. The Soviet Union has tended to favor international superpower management on a broader scale than has the United States in recent years, partly because its leaders are intensely power-oriented. Generally, and often with reason, Soviet spokesmen have shown their contempt for political formulas that ignore considerations of power and place important responsibilities in multiple, weak hands—unless the matter involved is of little consequence to them and there are propaganda advantages to be obtained.

Today, at great sacrifice, the Soviet Union is reaching military parity with the United States. It has both the capacity and will to defend a wide range of interests—unilaterally if necessary. For the Russians at this point multilateralism must thus be regarded as a tactic to be used sparingly on behalf of Soviet interests.

An alliance-accommodation system. Finally, there is the policy of accepting international involvement on a selective but extensive scale, reinforcing Soviet authority and power where possible by an alliance-accommodation system that cuts across Communist and non-Communist lines. Such a policy, as we have noted, exacts very considerable sacrifices from the Soviet people and involves risks, sometimes of sizable proportions. Moreover, it promises that crisis management will be a recurrent, time-consuming, nerve-wracking obligation thrust upon the Soviet system.

Nevertheless, it is virtually certain that Soviet foreign policy during the 1970s will be based primarily upon this approach. Why? Let us first explore further some general considerations bearing strongly upon Soviet attitudes and policies at this point. As we have indicated, the Soviet Union like the United States has global, albeit not universal, interests. Indeed, the emergence of the U.S.S.R. as a global power ranks as one of the most important political-strategic developments of the late twentieth century.

In many respects, moreover, Soviet power is still approaching its zenith, notwithstanding some increasing strictures upon its use that stem from what is referred to broadly as multipolarity. It is the juxtaposition of these two developments—emerging Soviet power and the restraints of multipolarity—that deserves attention, not merely the latter, as is so frequently the case in current analyses of the international order. Current "multipolar" trends require certain Soviet adjustments, now and in the future; however, they do not demand any abandonment of that central reliance upon power in its various forms which has constituted the hallmark of recent Soviet policy.

It is entirely possible that international developments underway will heighten the premium upon selectivity in making commitments. The Soviet Union may be required to live with a larger number of chaotic local situations or regional power vacuums than it has in the past without contemplating intervention. "Neutralism" in its strictest sense may acquire additional attraction in some situations for a nation hardpressed by other obligations. Within the spectrum of its global interests, however, the Pacific-Asian region as a general unit is certain to occupy a position of very high importance for the Soviet Union, second only to the importance of Europe.

Indeed, if Soviet desires with respect to Europe are largely satisfied in the near future, as seems possible, the Pacific-Asian region may assume first importance to the Russians. Moscow has good reason to be pleased with current developments on the European front. Since World War II, the major Soviet demand upon the West has been acceptance of the status quo established as a result of that war. Step by step, that acceptance has been attained. Moreover, European security arrangements, viewed from Soviet eyes, constitute less and less of a threat. East Europe, ironically, may pose greater problems for the U.S.S.R. than West Europe in the years immediately ahead. In general, however, the primary threats to Soviet security as well as the foremost political challenges are likely to come from Asia in the decade of the 1970s, and even more so in the 1980s, thereby making this the region of first concern to Moscow.

Given the geopolitics of the Eurasian continent, this challenge cannot be met by withdrawal. Nor would a holy crusade on behalf of the true faith be a realistic endeavor. The Soviet Union is ruled today by third generation "revolutionaries" who have grown grey in the service of a massive, stodgy, conservative bureaucracy. In speeches and through the Soviet media, they keep the Cold War alive even now, and leave ample space for attacks upon the Maoist heretics of the East. But their heart is in revolution only as it serves directly to undermine those whom they oppose or demonstrably to augment their own authority.

Russian leaders can be satisfied at this point only with an intricate, comprehensive policy that seeks to construct a large network of relations in Asia whose objective would be to maximize Soviet flexibility and power, and facilitate an effective defensive-offensive program against China and other "hostile" or competitive forces. Some of these relations will take the form of alliances, with heavy commitments. Others will involve "special ties" or close but partial interaction, tailored to specific requirements. Some will be no more than "normal" relations, with efforts made to neutralize potentially hostile forces.

In this quest for additional power and support, to what sources are the Soviets turning primarily? Japan is an obvious possibility, as we have seen. Closer Soviet-Japanese relations might provide not only for the more rapid development of the economically and strategically vital Siberia, but pose China with additional restraints. There are difficult problems to be resolved or contained, however, if such a relationship is to ensue. The psychological-political background of Russian-Japanese relations is strongly negative. Moreover, the Soviet Union must be prepared to make certain territorial concessions if it is to obtain Japanese cooperation—concessions possibly setting dangerous precedents, given the border problems with China and in East Europe. Nonetheless, closer Soviet-Japanese relations offer sufficient mutual advantage to make this a highly probable development, should rational considerations prevail.

It is with India, however, that the Soviet Union has thus far struck its closest bonds, at least among major Asian societies. The Soviet-

Indian relationship today represents an alliance as we have noted, despite Prime Minister Gandhi's disclaimers. Politically, militarily and economically, Russia is deeply committed to India and its client state, Bangladesh. India's striking victory in the most recent war with Pakistan redounded to Soviet prestige as well. But Soviet responsibilities—and the attendant risks—in the South Asian subcontinent, both of a short-range and long-range type, increased correspondingly. Now the Russians are learning, as did the Americans before them, of the high costs of victory in the world of international politics.

Conceivably, the Soviet-Indian alliance could prove onerous to one or both sides. Extensive military assistance to this massive nation will not be inexpensive, and the tasks of economic development confronting India are almost as colossal as those facing China. How much aid the Soviet leaders will wish, or be forced to give in the years ahead remains unclear. Moreover, Indian reactions to this alliance are not predictable, especially over the long run. Surely, Russia does not wish to repeat its experiences with Egypt. At this point, however, the Soviet-Indian alliance is evaluated positively by the Russians. The Indian domestic political climate is generally favorable to them, and the costs have been modest in comparison with the gains. The Indians now appear to be in a position to dominate the subcontinent and to contain China effectively along the entire Himalayan frontier. Meanwhile, the Russians have greatly increased their presence in the Indian Ocean, and on the subcontinent itself.

How far is the Soviet Union prepared to go in an accommodation with the United States in Asia? Obviously, no Soviet-American alliance is in the offing. On the contrary, the one hot war now raging, Vietnam, has had some of the characteristics of a war by proxy between America and Russia. The North Vietnamese invasion of the South revealed the fact that, for a long time, the Russians have been furnishing the Vietnamese Communists with highly sophisticated weaponry suitable for offensive use. Presumably they have also provided the training for some of those who use it. Without this aid, indeed, the Communist offensive of 1972 could not have taken place. Moreover, there is no evidence at present that Moscow intends to take decisive steps in bringing about a political settlement of this war—unless and until Hanoi so requests—although there are indications that Moscow has advised Hanoi recently that the best opportunities for a political settlement optimally favorable to the Communists might be secured before the November 1972 presidential election in the United States.[21]

It has long been conjectured that Moscow would welcome a compromise settlement of the Indochina struggle, one leaving North Vietnam dependent upon the U.S.S.R. and robbing the Chinese of any credit for victory. Again, there is no hard evidence to support this conjecture. Moscow does want to thwart Peking in the Indochina region as elsewhere. There can be no other explanation for its continued presence in Phnom Penh and its refusal to recognize the Sihanouk government-in-exile. Sino-Soviet rivalry also extends deeply into the murky Vietnamese scene. But thus far, the North Vietnamese have generally been able to turn the conflict to their advantage, although they appear deeply troubled by the refusal of either Moscow or Peking to take risks on their behalf under the conditions of their major 1972 offensive and the U.S. response.

In sum, there are few signs that the Soviet Union is interested in any accommodation with the United States in Asia that would bring into serious question Moscow's allegiance to its allies or to those whom it hopes to woo away from China. On all issues, indeed, including those involving direct U.S.-U.S.S.R. relations and Europe, the Russians have shown themselves to be exceedingly tough bargainers, dealing always from strength and making no unilateral concessions. From all indications, therefore, Soviet-American cooperation in Asia will be exceedingly limited during the foreseeable future and will be essentially a by-product of an independent Soviet assessment of its interests.

At the same time, the Soviet Union shows no hesitation in making overtures to a number of smaller non-Communist Asian states, offering normalized diplomatic relations, trade, cultural exchange, and other forms of intercourse. Indeed, such overtures have been extended to every nation in Southeast Asia. (Soviet policies in this respect have even prompted South Korea to try its luck—thus far without results.) In the case of Burma, Russia, armed with the Indian accord, is making new offers to support the beleaguered Ne Win government. In the case of Singapore, it has indicated an interest in the use of naval facilities. In Malaysia, significant rubber purchases are the hallmark of Soviet inter-

---

[21] It is reliably reported that this was the gist of Soviet President Nicolai Podgorny's message when he visited Hanoi in the summer of 1972. It has also been indicated that the response given him by the North Vietnamese leaders was cool, at least on the surface.

est. To Indonesia, the U.S.S.R. has displayed remarkable cooperation despite the strongly anti-Communist policies of the Suharto government. The Russians even appeared to cast a flirtatious wink at Taiwan in the form of allowing Victor Louis, newsman and frequently used Soviet conduit, to visit the island several years ago.

In June 1969, Leonid Brezhnev, secretary-general of the Communist party of the Soviet Union, called enigmatically for the creation of a "collective security system" in Asia in terms indicating that the containment of China had become the central item on the Soviet agenda and that Russia intended to play a major role in Asia. The Brezhnev appeal, clearly directed against Peking, not Washington, was initially greeted with mixed astonishment and silence from the intended respondents, but more recently it has been reiterated in somewhat different form by both Soviet and Indian sources. Meanwhile, the Soviet Union continues to pursue the containment of China, in a policy that mixes sheer power (nearly a million soldiers on the Sino-Soviet frontier and vast supplies of war equipment) with an intensive diplomacy that overlooks no one.

Clearly, the Soviet Union will continue to be a major force in the Pacific-Asian area. Indeed, until recently, its credibility as a power was at an all-time high throughout the area, as we have noted. The U.S.S.R. has not as yet suffered any discernible political-military defeats in East or South Asia, nor have the forces aligned with it. Moreover, there are no gaping wounds on the home front, at least none that can be seen by an outside observer.

These facts do not mean that the U.S.S.R. is universally admired. On the contrary, sentiments of fear, suspicion and hatred abound, as we have noted, and they deeply influence the policies of such countries as the People's Republic of China. In some measure, this is always a part of the cost of power. Nonetheless, the Soviet Union will rigorously uphold its interests, as defined by its ruling elite, and it will negotiate from strength. Despite the repeated charges from Peking that the two "superpowers" are engaged in a conspiracy to manage the world, a plot that infringes upon the sovereignty of all other states, the U.S.S.R. and the U.S. are far from having reached a cooperative relationship in Asia. Its great concern with China notwithstanding, the U.S.S.R. has no desire to see the United States powerful or successful in the Far East. It has worked mightily for an American defeat in Vietnam, albeit one that would not provide the Chinese with increased strength in Southeast

Asia. Moreover, its operations in South Asia, climaxed by its all-out support for India in the recent Indo-Pakistan war over Bangladesh, have been generally contrary to the policies and actions of the United States. Nor have the Russians shown any interest as yet in broadly based on cooperation in Northeast Asia, whether the issue is Korea, Taiwan, or the region as a whole.

On certain important issues, however, there are a few signals that future accommodation, or even cooperation, might be possible. For example, at the time of the Pueblo affair and again when an American reconnaissance plane was shot down over North Korea, the Soviet Union indicated by its behavior that it did not want another major round of hostilities in this region. While the Russians publicly back Peking on the Taiwan issue, their private position is less clear. Laos and Cambodia also represent a region where Soviet policy appears to have some flexibility, primarily because of Moscow's rivalry with Peking—although Russian commitments in this region do not appear to be extensive, and in general, seem subordinate to the desire to stay in step with North Vietnam.

These signals, while weak, suggest the range of interests which the U.S.S.R. and the U.S. potentially or actually hold in common in the Pacific-Asian area. Those common interests include the avoidance of direct confrontation; the desire to prevent China from acquiring a large sphere of influence or control beyond its own borders; agreements that will cut the risks of local wars, especially those fought among the major powers by proxy, risking larger conflicts; agreements upon arms control, including control of nuclear weapons, in which the Chinese among others would be parties; and finally, an interest in preserving the status quo in Asia, while enlarging the "neutralized" regions where no single major power would have sole or dominant influence.

Let it be emphasized that at the moment, some of these interests are more potential than operative. In addition, it is not likely that these interests are or will be held with the same intensity by the two superpowers. Hence, both priorities and policies will differ. Finally, whatever commitment the Soviet Union may make to the Asian status quo as it considers the costs and risks of alternatives, if revolutions or upheavals appear to advance Soviet influence or prestige, Moscow will not hesitate to abet them, defending its actions in the name of "proletarian internationalism."

The United States: The Trauma of Power

Let us now turn to the second "superpower" in the Pacific-Asian region, the United States. It is interesting to recall that the United States first went to Asia because of poverty, not affluence. In the aftermath of the Revolutionary War, the new American nation was cut off from the markets of Great Britain and the British Empire. Merchant ships and seamen were idled, and fresh sources of trade became a dire necessity. The first American contacts with Asia stemmed from these facts.

The Roots of America's Asian Policies. Throughout the nineteenth century, American involvement in East Asia was minimal and directed largely toward economic objectives. The United States was a minor power, and one with very limited interests in international affairs. Its energies were largely absorbed in opening and developing a continent. Washington's injunction to avoid "entangling alliances" seemed to fit the needs of a young nation fully occupied with the tasks of assimilating great waves of immigrants from highly diverse lands and exploiting the extraordinary resources with which its land was blessed. The Monroe Doctrine was more a part of, than apart from, a policy that had many of the hallmarks of isolationism. To declare the Western hemisphere off limits to further European "encroachment" was one method of seeking to keep the quarrels of the "old world" distant from American shores. That its thrust was also to create an American "sphere of influence" was a secondary consideration, at least initially.

In this era the case for isolationism was strong. On either side of the American continent, a huge ocean separated the United States from all of the major powers and principal problems of the time. To the north and south were sparsely populated, nonexpansionist states. Threats to American security from external sources, therefore, were minimal. Moreover, there was no great need for the resources of foreign lands. The American economy was as self-sufficient in this period as the economy of any developing society.

Meanwhile, internal challenges were mounting. Sectional and regional differences tended to grow rather than diminish, products of the different stages of development, the different economies, and the different social structures characterizing the American North, South and West. In the rapidly expanding cities, great ethnic blocs were being

61

formed with bitter antagonisms frequently erupting. The task of nation-building was certain to be lengthy and painful, as the Civil War was to demonstrate so conclusively.

In the opening stages, therefore, American policies in Asia were largely the policies of dependency. The United States frequently took its lead from the actions and attitudes of the major Western powers, and especially from Great Britain, foremost power of the period. The principal interest of the United States revolved around having access to Asian trade on the same basis as other states. Hence, "most favored nation treatment" became the basic element in U.S. Asian policy, leading to the later charge that what others took by force, the United States then insisted upon acquiring as a right.

From the beginning, however, the United States displayed a strong interest in upholding the sovereignty of such states as China and Japan, and took a generally hostile position toward the establishment of European colonies and spheres of influence in Asia. The reasons were primarily economic: the Europeans tended to restrict if not make impossible foreign trade in regions under their control. But political objections were also expressed. The United States, itself an ex-colony and without need of empire, generally favored such principles as self-determination and independence.

By the close of the nineteenth century, however, three basic dilemmas had appeared in America's Asian policies. The first pertained to the question of unilateralism versus collective action. Should the United States chart its own policies and pursue those policies aloof from others? In this period, "others" normally referred to other Western states. The chief actors on the Asian scene were European states, the "acted upon" were Asian societies. The arguments for unilateralism stemmed from the differences in American objectives, hence policies. Given its more limited interests, moreover, why should the United States undertake the risks and costs of collective action? On the other hand, if it eschewed such action, how could its interests, and those whom it supported, be upheld?

Closely tied with this dilemma was another: In seeking to achieve its objectives, should the United States place primary reliance upon moral suasion, or upon some type of sanctions involving political, economic or military action? Could moral suasion suffice to achieve agreements, and subsequently, to ensure their faithful execution? If not, was the United States, alone or in concert with others, prepared to pay the costs of some type of sanctions?

A final dilemma was more subtle: What role did the United States seek to play in Asia and, more importantly perhaps, what role or roles was it actually playing? The American impact, along with that of other "advanced" Western states, was generally a revolutionary one in Asia. American values, institutions, and way of life all tore at the traditional fabric of Asian society. Much of this impact was unplanned, even unconscious. Yet, by means of missionaries, traders, seamen and other travellers, and through books, schools and technology, the West in general and the United States in particular posed an unprecedented challenge, especially to Asian elites. At the same time, however, official American policy was directed primarily toward upholding existing governments in Asia and advancing political stability. Thus Americans were, at one and the same time, revolutionaries and upholders of the status quo.

None of these dilemmas was fully resolved in the period prior to World War II. In general, the United States pursued a unilateral course in Asia, with only occasional efforts at collective action. Befitting a commitment to minimal risk policies, moreover, its primary reliance throughout the period was upon moral suasion. Only after World War II had begun were serious economic sanctions applied. It was then too late, and these led to a larger war, involving the United States itself. The contradictory impact of the United States in Asia also continued, with contributions being made simultaneously to revolution and the status quo.

Increasingly, the arguments for isolationism seemed outdated, but a position deeply entrenched in both culture and policy was not quickly or easily changed. As a result of the Spanish-American War, the United States had acquired possessions not merely in the mid-Pacific but in East Asia as well. From this point, its political-strategic interests in the Pacific-Asian area began to equal, then surpass, its economic interests. Meanwhile, technology on all fronts was advancing—in industry, communications and weaponry—bringing Asia as well as Europe ever closer to America.

The effort to prevent Japan from extending its hegemony over East Asia, however, failed. The loosely knit multilateral policies fashioned at the Washington Conference of 1921-22 proved totally ineffective, and no meaningful policies, collective or unilateral, were created

63

during the 1930s to replace them. On the contrary, having finally made a full commitment to internationalism in the midst of World War I, the United States had once again withdrawn from effective participation, midst disillusionment and mutual recriminations. Within a decade, moreover, the Great Depression struck and attention was heavily concentrated upon domestic problems.

It was during this time that men like Senator Gerald Nye defined the causes of war by placing the responsibility heavily upon munition-makers and other "profit-seekers." The physical presence of Americans in belligerent zones was also blamed, along with the general involvement of the United States in the international scene. The so-called Neutrality Acts followed, products of a tragic misunderstanding of the nature of the contemporary world.

World War II soon broke out. The isolationists were swept away, repudiated by events in as stark and decisive a fashion as was imaginable. But the costs of isolationism were now paid in resources and lives. Nevertheless, such a war summoned up a total commitment fully in accord with American culture. Moreover, total war yielded total victory, and the United States emerged at the end of the war as the world's indisputable first power.

Premises Underlying Postwar Policies. It is against this background that the initial postwar Asian policies of the United States took shape. Four premises characterized American thinking about Asia as the war came to a close.

First, China, unified and led by the Nationalists, would emerge as the dominant nation of Asia and serve as a symbol both for economic development and for an era of Asian peace and independence. Aided by the United States and committed to the path of democracy, China would become the linchpin in America's Asian policies.

Second, the United States and the Soviet Union would be able to preserve their wartime working relations, finding means of cooperation on all major issues, both in Europe and Asia.

Third, Japan had first to be punished for its militarist, aggressive policies of the past, then put firmly on the path of democracy and pacifism, so that it would never again menace Asia.

Finally, the decolonization of South and Southeast Asia would take place relatively quickly and smoothly. Most of the newly independent governments of the region, moreover, would be dedicated to parliamentarism in the Western mold and to playing a constructive role in the international arena.

None of these premises proved to be valid. Within a few years, the Communists had toppled the Nationalists in China and had entered into an alliance with the Soviet Union, proclaiming themselves to be staunchly loyal members of the Communist bloc. Cooperation between the United States and the Soviet Union broke down over such critical issues as Poland, Berlin and Greece in Europe, Korea and Japan in Asia. Indeed, within a few years, the Cold War began, with barriers being thrown up everywhere, physical and political alike. In Asia, the Stalinists were calling for guerrilla warfare along a wide front, once again seeking to wed nationalism and communism in the service of the latter. Shortly, moreover, a hot war was to be launched by the Communists in Korea, at huge cost to all parties concerned.

Under these circumstances, the vision of a weak, pastoral, pacifist Japan became far less attractive. In rapid succession, the United States moved through three phases in its policies toward Japan: an initial emphasis upon punishment and reform; then concentration upon economic rehabilitation and recovery; and, third, a proffered alliance, with Japan being encouraged to acquire a capacity for self-defense.

Finally, decolonization proved to be neither quick nor easy for many parts of southern Asia. European intransigence joined with indigenous cleavages and weaknesses to render Indonesia and Vietnam full-fledged battlefields. Even where formal independence in southern Asia came quickly, the tasks of nation-building and economic development proved enormously difficult. Political fragility and economic backwardness thus combined to make many areas available for external influence. This situation was accelerated, moreover, by Europe's abrupt withdrawal from some regions, its dogged determination to hold its positions in others.

"Revisionism" and the Record—The Current Debate Over the Past.
Finding its initial premises faulty, the United States was forced to reconsider many of its Asian policies in the years immediately after 1945, and to reverse some of them. In certain quarters today, it is fashionable to blame the United States for the tension and militancy that emerged in the late 1940s. A group of "revisionists," some of them academicians and journalists, some of them politicians (and their research assistants), have sought to rewrite the history of this era to place primary responsi-

bility for the collapse of East-West relations, both in Europe and in Asia, upon America. ·

The thrust of their writings can be summarized in the form of the questions they raise: Could we not have cooperated with the Communists in China rather than aiding only the Nationalists, thereby offering the Chinese Communists an alternative to Soviet aid and, at the same time, accommodating the United States to the New China at the time of its emergence? Was the Cold War not a product of the deep, unreasoning fear of communism that warped American thought and action after 1945? Was the United States not wrong to shift the Japanese from the path of pacifism to which it had initially committed them? Did it not fail to support nationalism in Asia, particularly nationalism flying Communist banners, thereby confining American aid to corrupt, backward governments, incapable of sustaining themselves? Did not U.S. policies of containing communism in the Pacific-Asian area place undue emphasis upon military approaches to socioeconomic and political problems, and result in a series of paper treaties and alliances, with all of the bone and sinew having to be provided by the American people? [22]

This is not the place to evaluate these questions in great detail, but since they bear strongly upon current policy alternatives, some attention must be given to each. Turning to the China problem first, in point of fact, while rejecting earlier proposals from certain American officials for a closer relation with the Chinese Communists (including the provision of some assistance), the United States did attempt, by the time of George Marshall's mission to China in 1946, a fairly even-handed policy based upon the thesis that China should have a coalition government, with Nationalists and Communists cooperating with each other.[23]

---

[22] Recent revisionist writings would include Richard Barnet, *Intervention and Revolution: The United States in the Third World* (New York: World Publishing Co., 1968); Barton J. Bernstein, ed., *Towards a New Past* (New York: Pantheon Books, 1969); Edward Friedman and Mark Selden, eds., *America's Asia: Dissenting Essays on Asian-American Relations* (New York: Pantheon Books, 1971); Philip Green and Sanford Levinson, eds., *Power and Community* (New York: Pantheon Books, 1970); and Theodore Roszak, ed., *The Dissenting Academy* (New York: Pantheon Books, 1968). While only the Friedman-Selden collection of essays pertains specifically to Asia, the general themes of the other works are pertinent to our discussion here.

For an earlier work of a similar nature, see William A. Williams, *The Tragedy of American Diplomacy* (New York: Dell Publishing Co., 1962).

[23] For details of this period, see Herbert Feis, *The China Tangle: The American Effort in China from Pearl Harbor to the Marshall Mission* (Princeton, New Jersey: Princeton University Press, 1953); and the recent work of Barbara Tuch-

Heavy pressure was put on the Nationalists at certain points during this critical period, and General Marshall ended his mission with his famous "plague on both your houses" dictum, indicating disgust with both of the principal Chinese parties.[24] The problem with American policy was that it was based upon an unreal proposition, namely, that coalition government was plausible or even possible. China was not West Europe, and there was nothing in its recent political history to indicate that coalition was a feasible approach. Only the absence of any other promising solution could possibly excuse the optimism that prevailed on this matter.

When Chinese Communist victory became an established fact, the United States did signal unmistakably its intention to accept that victory and to establish normal relations with the new government in Peking. What such an event would have meant to subsequent international relations in Asia cannot be known because Peking's new leaders made it clear in a variety of ways that they were not interested in American recognition. Indeed, incidents perpetrated upon our consulates in Mukden and Shanghai appeared to be deliberate actions, officially approved, to make rapid recognition impossible.[25] Then the Korean War followed shortly.

U.S. relations with the People's Republic of China since 1949 provide an excellent illustration of a central maxim in international relations: basic policy changes in the relations between and among states can only be consummated at certain times. In point of fact, rather infrequent opportunities for such change present themselves. When those opportunities arise, moreover, the parties centrally involved must both (all) be prepared to support change, seeing it in their respective interests to do so.

In its first years, the People's Republic of China had no interest in American recognition. During the Korean War and its immediate aftermath, no significant change in Sino-American relations was possible. In

man, *Stillwell and the American Experience in China* (New York, The Macmillan Co., 1970). For the Kuomintang point of view, see Chiang Kai-shek, *Soviet Russia in China: A Summing Up at Seventy* (New York: Farrar, Straus and Cudahy, 1957); and Chin-tung Liang, *General Stilwell in China, 1942-1944: The Full Story* (Jamaica, New York: St. John's University Press, 1972).

[24] The American official position is set forth in the so-called White Paper issued by the U.S. Department of State during the Truman era entitled "United States Relations with China" (Washington, D.C.: U.S. Government Printing Office, 1949).

[25] Ibid., pp. 318-323.

the mid-fifties, the possibility of a change was signalled by Peking, but American policies did not permit a positive response at this point, and a series of crises in the Taiwan Straits then ensued.[26] Beginning in 1961, however, when the United States showed a new flexibility, Peking's position had become rigid; the P.R.C. insisted that absolutely no change in relations could take place unless and until the Taiwan issue was settled to its satisfaction. Only a full decade later, for reasons already discussed, did the leaders of the People's Republic shift their position, enabling an official American-Chinese dialogue to commence.

There is certainly no evidence to sustain the thesis that the United States could have turned the Chinese Communists into Titoists, let alone liberals, in the 1940s had it offered aid and wooed them with other concessions. To read *Chih-fang Jih-pao* (Liberation Daily), the Communist organ for this period, is to see how deeply committed the Maoists were to communism *and* to a Stalinist view of the world. It is naive in the extreme to believe that *before their experience with the Russians,* Mao and his associates could have been caused to abandon them by the American government. Indeed, even after those experiences, the Sino-Soviet break was a long, painful, divisive process that produced deep fissures within Chinese Communist ranks.

As for the broader question of responsibility for the Cold War, Korea serves as an excellent case study of the type of issue that created tension between the Americans and Russians, a case study drawn from Asia but with parallels in Europe. In August 1945, neither the United States nor the U.S.S.R. had any intention of seeing Korea permanently divided. The 38th parallel was established merely as a temporary line to separate the respective occupational forces until the principles governing a unified state could be determined. In the months that followed, strenuous efforts were made to reach agreement on those principles. Failure was not due to trivial causes.[27]

The central issue was nothing less than who should control Korea. The Soviet negotiators were insistent upon defining those who could participate in the organization of a Korean government in such a fashion as to ensure Communist control. The Americans were equally insis-

---

[26] For details, see A. Doak Barnett, *Communist China and Asia: Challenge to American Policy* (New York: Harper and Row, 1960).

[27] For details, see Robert A. Scalapino and Chong-Sik Lee, *Communism in Korea,* vol. 1 (Berkeley: University of California Press, 1972), chapters IV and V.

tent that this not happen, knowing that once the Communists came to power, any changes via free elections were impossible. The basic issue was similar in other parts of the world, including Poland, Czechoslovakia, and Germany. Where the Communists could not hope to manipulate the political processes to their advantage peacefully, moreover, they did not hesitate to use force. Indeed, by 1947-48, the Cominform was calling openly for guerrilla warfare throughout the world, and in cases where it was feasible, such as Greece, the Communists were providing extensive assistance to the guerrillas. Those who now maintain that the United States was primarily responsible for the Cold War have an obligation to face these and other facts, and to assess the alternative policies which Washington might have pursued.

Naturally, these developments affected U.S. policies and attitudes toward Japan. Initially, the Russians had wanted to share in the Japanese occupation and, had that occurred, one more divided state would now exist in Asia. The Soviet Union continued to favor a very tough policy against Japan throughout the occupational years, one which would have negated any possibility of Japanese economic recovery.[28] The United States quickly saw that this would put 80 million people on a permanent American dole. It also saw that dire poverty and experimentation in democracy were not compatible. The American occupation was formally ended much earlier than had originally been planned, but the San Francisco Treaty of 1951 was flatly rejected by the Communist bloc, leaving Japan still technically at war with the Soviet Union and its allies. The Korean War, moreover, was still exacting a heavy toll. Thus, wars both hot and cold were underway. It is not surprising,

---

[28] The occupation era is covered by a number of books, from a variety of viewpoints. See Frederick S. Dunn, *Peacemaking and the Settlement with Japan* (Princeton, N.J.: Princeton University Press, 1963); Robert A. Fearey, *The Occupation of Japan—Second Phase: 1948-50* (New York: Macmillan Books, 1950); Herbert Passin, ed., *United States and Japan,* The American Assembly Series (Englewood Cliffs, N.J.: Prentice-Hall, 1966); Edwin O. Reischauer, *The United States and Japan,* 3d ed. (Cambridge, Mass.: Harvard University Press, 1965); William Sebald, *With MacArthur in Japan* (New York: W. W. Norton & Co., Inc., 1965); Supreme Commander for the Allied Powers, *Political Reorientation of Japan, September 1945 to September 1948,* Report of the Government Section, 2 vols. (Westport, Conn.: Greenwood Press, Inc., 1949); Robert E. Ward, "Reflections on the Allied Occupation and Planned Political Change in Japan," in Robert E. Ward, ed., *Political Development in Modern Japan* (Princeton, N.J.: Princeton University Press, 1968), and Courtney Whitney, *MacArthur: His Rendezvous with History* (New York: Alfred A. Knopf, Inc., 1956).

therefore, that issues of security were of significance for the United States and for the Japanese leaders as well.

Meanwhile, American policy toward colonial Asia satisfied neither the European powers involved nor the more ardent nationalist leaders of the area. There is merit in the view that Washington did not apply sufficient pressure to such colonial powers as France to reach an early, equitable settlement with moderate nationalists, thereby reducing the risks that nationalist movements would be captured by extremists. Clearly, French colonial policies in the post-1945 era were shortsighted and, in the end, led to disastrous results. One needs only to contrast French attitudes and actions in southern Asia with those of the British to note the very substantial difference in results.

Nevertheless, at critical points the United States did apply extensive pressure upon Europeans, did offer its good offices, and did adopt general policies that favored the nationalist cause in colonial Asia. Indeed, the Dutch and more particularly, the French never forgave the Americans for some of those actions. It is a favorite French assertion that the United States undermined their position in Southeast Asia— and then inherited it. From the outset of the postwar period, the United States tended to regard European colonialism in Asia as outmoded, and generally urged a rapid liquidation of colonial rule. Later, American policies became more complex and less consistent as U.S. policy makers developed a concern about the Communist role in southern Asia and the enormous troubles that followed rapid decolonization in many Asian regions. However, at no point was the United States prepared to use its military forces to uphold European control in Asia and, in a number of cases, its European allies accused it of consciously helping to destroy their positions, such as in Indonesia and Indochina.

This leads into certain broader issues that still impinge heavily upon American attitudes, including the attitudes of the academic community. Asian nationalism is frequently treated as if it were a uniform movement politically, invariably mass-supported and mass-based, and consistently "good." From these false premises the extremely dubious conclusion is drawn that if the United States would only support Asian nationalism, the success of its policies would be assured.

In point of fact, almost all organized political movements and would-be political leaders in postwar Asia fly nationalist banners. The political spectrum covered by these "nationalists" ranges from highly traditionalist, anti-modern, religious-based movement to the self-

70

proclaimed Marxist-Leninists who insist that they are first and foremost internationalists. Nationalists have killed nationalists throughout Asia, and they are still doing so.

Asian nationalism, moreover, remains largely an elitist phenomenon, at least if we use that term in a strict political sense. Antiforeignism, to be sure, is deeply rooted in many cultures—in the fear of the unknown, the outside, and the different. But these same attitudes can be applied to ethnic groups *within* a new state. Indeed, one of the most perplexing, unsolved problems confronting the new leaders of this area has been how much political and cultural autonomy to grant to diverse ethnic groups not in the main stream. In general, the nation-building process has only begun in southern Asia. Political allegiances are still given first to the primordial levels of authority, and commitments to the nation-state and its principal institutions are secondary, vague and uncertain. Where national loyalties do exist, they tend to focus upon the Leader, be he monarch or revolutionary. Personalization of loyalty invariably precedes institutionalization—hence, the strong tendency toward a cult of personality in Communist as well as certain non-Communist emerging states.

In postwar Asia, probably nationalism in its modern, Western sense has been most deeply implanted in China and North Korea. Here, mass mobilization and indoctrination have been intensive. The central themes have included patriotism, an unquestioning allegiance to party and leader, a willingness to work and fight for the motherland, and a strong belief in the superiority of the new national values and institutions.

Is this "good?" In broad terms, it is conducive to the same opportunities and dangers that have been a product of Western nationalism in the past several centuries. Unity can produce material progress and an expanded commitment to the common welfare. It can also produce a complex of power and emotionalism susceptible to exploitation for aggressive purposes. Obviously, it must be a matter for external concern if the citizens of any given state are taught to hate designated opponents with a blind fury and to revere all that is epitomized by their own political-economic system with an indiscriminate passion, particularly if they are being molded into citizen-soldiers. Thus, the question for the United States is not whether to support Asian nationalism, but what forms and types of Asian nationalism to support, and in what manner.

The issue of U.S. support for "corrupt dictatorships" is often encased in premises as simplistic as those underwriting the appeal for an undifferentiated support of Asian nationalism. One does not need to endorse all American policies, or leave unchallenged all American decisions concerning support, in order to raise some very fundamental questions about the manner in which the argument concerning "corrupt dictatorships" is customarily put.

Without exception, corruption is a serious problem in the open and quasi-open societies of Asia. In point of fact, as is well known, it is a problem of varying degree in all such societies, including the United States and other "advanced" Western states. In some measure, unfortunately, freedom and corruption go together. When individuals are allowed to operate freely, without rigid regulation, they will display a wide range of behavior patterns, some of them venal and anti-social. No one should be oblivious to this problem, nor shrink from the attack upon it. External aid or assistance, moreover, should constantly be scrutinized to see whether it is actually abetting such corruption, and what type of safeguards might be desirable. But what critics often leave unsaid is that rigidly authoritarian societies also breed corruption, albeit of special types. Are not the requirements imposed upon the intellectual in such a system one painful example? Should this preclude all forms of American aid or interaction with such regimes?

Dictatorship is a word often thrown around loosely in the political marketplace. It should be readily acknowledged, however, that few if any emerging societies are equipped to operate Western-style democracy in a fashion deemed satisfactory to most Americans. Once again, should the criterion for extending U.S. aid be that the recipient societies must meet American democratic standards? Such a position would surely represent an intense form of ethnocentrism. U.S. international assistance would quickly end, except for a few "advanced" states, mostly European. But more importantly, such a position ignores factors of supreme importance, namely, the difference of degree with respect to political rights currently existing between quasi-open and closed societies. Contrary to some assertions, there is a major difference in these respects between Seoul and P'yŏngyang, Saigon and Hanoi, merely to take two prominent examples. Moreover, there may also be an equally important difference in their respective potential for political evolution. The movement away from the mass-mobilized, one-party dictatorship and the police state which it tends to foster would appear to be exceedingly difficult.

Alternatives for U.S. Policy in Asia. Irrespective of how one evaluates American policies in postwar Asia, and how one conceptualizes such forces as nationalism, communism and modernization, it must be agreed that the United States currently stands at an important crossroads with respect to its Asian policies. Three broad alternatives now confront this nation. While we shall present them initially in "pure" form, in reality, as in the case of other nations, these alternatives are not mutually exclusive, and the concrete issue is likely to be what policy mix ultimately evolves.

A minimal foreign policy. One alternative, which would represent the new isolationism, is withdrawal. While a few new themes have been added, the arguments for it bear a remarkable similarity to those made for isolationism before World War II: the pressing importance of domestic problems and the need to concentrate America's full energies upon them; Asia's lack of importance to the security interests of the United States, and America's ability to sustain itself both economically and politically without deep involvement in the Asian scene; the high risks and extensive costs connected with any alliance or involvement pattern, as exemplified by the Korean and Vietnam wars; and finally, the inability of the United States to understand Asia, the successive failures of its efforts, and the antagonisms of Asians, including those Asians the U.S. is trying to help, that result from American policies.

The arguments against a withdrawal policy are also in the main familiar, since the debate is not a new one—although once again, additional themes have emerged. Let us briefly summarize these arguments, a number of which have already been introduced: total concentration upon domestic problems is a false conception, since it is neither possible nor, if attempted, would it accomplish the objectives desired; a reexamination of priorities on both the foreign and domestic fronts is always in order, but the all-in/all-out syndrome is a mark of immaturity, and can ony lead to repeated crises; both in economic and political terms, the United States is becoming more interdependent with the rest of the world, as the growth of multinational corporations, foreign investment, trade volume, and international communications of all types illustrates; indeed, the lines between "domestic" and "international"

73

politics are ever more difficult to define and maintain; in the area of security as well, with the advent of "spy-in-the-sky" satellites, nuclear-powered submarines, and a host of other long-range weapons, U.S. defense is intimately connected with the general world order; and the age when a garrison America would suffice has long since passed into history.

It is further argued that the problems of peaceful coexistence and weapons control, while not restricted to a single region, take on particular significance in the Pacific-Asian theater due to the physical presence there of the U.S.S.R., the People's Republic of China and the United States—in addition to Japan, India, and a host of other important societies. Admittedly, the risks of involvement are high, and the price Americans have paid for it has been heavy, but U.S. expenditures can now be reduced as a result of recent developments, and unilateralism can give way to an increased sharing of burdens. Finally, the risks of withdrawal in the long run far outweigh those of participation, especially in the age which is now beginning.

The debate over withdrawal versus participation, like most other major political debates, will not be determined by "rational" factors alone. There can be little doubt that a deep isolationist mood is abroad among the American people today. In part, it is the result of the frustrations connected with the two limited wars in which Americans have recently been involved, those of Korea and Vietnam. In part, it is a testimony to the extraordinary revolution through which the United States has been passing, a continuous revolution underway for decades, the product of spectacular economic-technological growth. That revolution has no parallel in the contemporary world in terms of its impact upon the mobility, living standards, life style and values of the average citizen. Not even the Japanese revolution to which we earlier referred has yet acquired the same intensity. Correspondingly, it has bequeathed monumental problems as the world's first post-modern society searches for new approaches to a new situation. Finally, the isolationist mood is also a product of timing. After a quarter of a century of intensive commitment to the world, the American is tired of sacrifice, less hopeful of solutions and, above all, weary of crisis.

The influence of the media upon this mood cannot be overlooked. By defining news as the most sensational event of the moment, the media are automatically involved in massive and continuous distortion. The atmosphere of constant crisis and impending doom projected by the media ultimately influences public attitudes, particularly those involving any degree of participation; and withdrawal provides a sense of deep psychological relief. Correction of this bias does not appear to be in sight. Under present conditions, the news media operate as a form of entertainment, in competition with other types of entertainment for a mass audience. Consequently, the bizarre, the extreme and, above all, the "bad" receive exposure out of all proportion to their intrinsic importance, while the developmental, the subtle, the complex and the "good" receive far less attention than a balanced treatment of events would warrant.

To combat the "bad" and to resist the gloomy, government inevitably seeks to engage in its own news management in increasing degree. The result is an antagonistic and almost ritualistic dance between the media and the government, with spiraling charges and countercharges. The citizen becomes confused, the credibility of both contestants is severely damaged, and the process tends to strengthen the public desire for relief.

There is reason to believe that all of the above factors have combined to create a powerful momentum for withdrawal, not only from Asia but from Europe and other areas as well. At the same time, however, this appears to be an issue upon which "elitist" and "mass" opinion exhibit important differences. Reflecting this fact, current governmental policies are probably much more geared to international participation than American public opinion is presently prepared to support. Such a situation, namely, a considerable gap beween policy and public opinion, is not unusual in the modern world. In a state as open and as democratic as the United States, however, that gap cannot be sustained indefinitely. Either events must serve to alter public opinion, or policies will be progressively adjusted to accord broadly with that opinion.

Multilateralism. Before assessing the prospects in this regard, let us examine a second alternative, reliance upon multilateralism. Such a policy would seek to replace most unilateral and bilateral actions or commitments with a wide range of multilateral activities. In the security field, primary attention would first be directed toward obtaining agreement from the principal Communist and non-Communist states to guarantee the security of such nations as Japan, North and South Korea (pending any agreement between the two parties on peaceful unification), and various states in Southeast Asia. Nuclear-free zones would be negotiated in conjunction with such guarantees. In this fashion, a new security system would emerge, replacing the old bilateral mutual security treaties currently in effect. Moreover, this system would be reinforced by a multilateral agreement on peaceful coexistence, including a stipulation of its essential requirements and the establishment of machinery whereby complaints could be heard and remedial action taken.

What if no such agreements could be reached with the Communist states? A fall-back position of the multilateral policy would be to confine new security arrangements to non-Communist states, but to scrap the old bilateral treaties in favor of broader, more comprehensive agreements, possibly including a Pacific-Asian security agreement, that would provide for the more equitable distribution of responsibilities.

In political matters, an attempt would be made to revitalize the United Nations, and at the same time to place additional emphasis upon regional groupings such as the Association of Southeast Asian Nations (ASEAN) and the Asian and Pacific Council (ASPAC), possibly enlarged. These regional organizations would undertake a wide range of consultative and cooperative functions, including possibly the primary responsibility for handling disputes strictly confined to the area itself and for forwarding complaints about external interference to the U.N. or some body of major powers.

In the economic arena, the United States would put its central effort into multilateral undertakings, both with respect to economic relations among advanced states and assistance programs to the late developing societies. The facilities of GATT would be fully utilized, possibly supplemented by the development of a Pacific community comprised initially of such states as the U.S., Japan, Canada, Australia and New Zealand. Critical negotiations concerning trade, investment and other issues among the major non-Communist states would take place in a multilateral environment and strictly bilateral agreements would be downgraded. U.S. aid programs would be funneled largely if not wholly through organizations like the World Bank and the Asian Development Bank, with special regional groups drawing up coordinated plans.

The arguments on behalf of such a policy are extremely persuasive. If it were successful, it would not only reduce the burdens which the United States has carried, often alone, but it would provide a hopeful new symbolism of international cooperation, thereby encouraging a weary American public to continue its involvement in world affairs. Moreover, such a policy puts certain critical issues in the only framework from which true progress can be expected. Most of the economic problems confronting the world, and particularly those involving the advanced industrial states, are not susceptible to unilateral or bilateral treatment. In the realm of security as well, without the ultimate participation of all of the major states including the leading Communist states, meaningful advances on such issues as weapons control and peaceful coexistence cannot be expected.

As America discovered after World War II, however, overenthusiasm for grandiose schemes that bear a limited relationship to the political realities of the world can result in great psychological depression when they fail, and it can also be dangerous. The world is still a very considerable distance from the type of international community that would enable the United States to place *central reliance* upon multilateralism, desirable although it may be to increase the amount of multilateralism in U.S. policy at this point. The value and institutional structures of the major states remain radically different, lending themselves to varying goals and types of political behavior. In particular, any policies resting upon the premise of symmetrical relations among the major powers today would rest upon false foundations. U.S. ties with certain states are destined to be much closer than those with others for a wide range of reasons, many of which we have already explored. Moreover, these relations will be different in type, from state to state.

It is essential that the United States avoid the fate of the loosely knit multilateral policies that were fashioned during the Washington Conference 50 years ago. If that is to be done, Washington will have to experiment cautiously with certain types of multilateralism even as it supports a rapid advance of multilateralism on other fronts.

An alliance-accommodation system. There remains the alternative closest to present American policies, namely, that of a modified alliance structure. The Nixon Doctrine represents such a policy in its initial phases. The United States would agree to maintain its commitments modifying certain treaties or arrangements with the mutual consent of the parties involved but not unilaterally. Each American ally, however, would be responsible for its own first-line defense in the event of an external attack. The United States would continue to furnish a nuclear umbrella as protection against major power involvement or

77

blackmail, but it would expect those nations allied with it to handle their internal security problems and any limited wars involving neighboring or regional forces. In the latter event, American air and sea power, but not ground forces, might be used in cases where an act of aggression had been determined. Fixed bases in populous areas of East Asia would no longer be manned by Americans. Rather, the U.S. base complex would center upon America's mid-Pacific possessions, with an additional heavy reliance upon mobile bases—that is, submarines and aircraft. Certain bases in allied countries would be kept at a readiness level by indigenous forces, available in the event of an attack or serious threat.

With what nations would such security prevail? In Northeast Asia, the bilateral arrangements with Japan, the Republic of Korea, and the Republic of China on Taiwan would continue unless the status of one of these states were to change, or alternate multilateral guarantees were to be approved by the governments concerned. In the Pacific, security ties would be maintained with Australia and New Zealand. In Southeast Asia, the United States would retain its commitments with the Philippines and Thailand. With respect to continental Southeast Asia, however, it would seek a neutralization agreement involving most if not all of the states in the region, an agreement adhered to by both the Soviet Union and the People's Republic of China.

The modified alliance structure sketched above represents a commitment beyond that favored by a sizable number of Americans, as we have noted, and it may face political difficulties, both in Congress and with the public at large. One cannot rule out the possibility, moreover, that an individual would be elected President who favored a withdrawal policy, or at least far greater steps in that direction than are contemplated under the modified alliance policy.

As in the case of Japan, emotional or psychological factors may intervene decisively in the process of American foreign policy formation in the period immediately ahead. However, if decisions are reached in an essentially rational fashion, with the data pertaining to international conditions analyzed as fully as possible and the available alternatives carefully scrutinized, the case for a modified alliance policy at this point is exceedingly strong.

The central task confronting the United States in the coming decade is that of balancing its responsibilities as the world's foremost revolutionary society with its responsibilities as one of the world's two most powerful nations. At present, the United States has a combination of power and flexibility in international affairs denied to all other nations. It stands at the apex of two triangles critical to the course of the 1970s and beyond.

The first of these triangles is the U.S.S.R.-U.S.-China triangle, so vital to the issues of peaceful coexistence and weapons control. If there is to be a broader climate of peace in the world, these issues must receive prompt and intensive attention. The risks of war among the major powers appear to have receded, in considerable part because the costs of nuclear war are too high to contemplate. It is entirely possible, however, that unless important changes are introduced, violence in the form of a multitude of undeclared, "limited" wars will increase. Some of these struggles, moreover, as in the past, will be wars among the major powers by proxy, with grave risks of escalation. Thus, it is essential that the big nations most centrally involved in this range of problems begin a dialogue on the fundamental questions that will determine the political-military climate of the future. How can peaceful coexistence be forwarded? What are its requirements, and how can they be attained, then patrolled? How can weapons control be achieved and if possible, mutual disarmament, in such a manner as to protect the security of all parties?

At the same time, a second triangle is of equal importance, that of Japan-U.S.-West Europe. Economic and political relations among these states will have a critical influence upon the economic and political health of the advanced and developing states alike. Some growth in economic relations between the Communist and non-Communist states is to be expected in the years immediately ahead, but the truly vital ties will continue to be those within the Japan-U.S.-West Europe triangle. It is here, indeed, that the mixed forces of internationalism, nationalism, and regionalism are moving forward in intricate, sometimes contradictory, fashion. With the advent of 1973, the U.S., Japan and the Western European states shall commence a new round of negotiations concerning tariff and non-tariff barriers, and a host of other issues, as we have earlier indicated.

Given these developments, American interests cannot be served by an attempt to return to isolationism, under whatever guise. Adjustments in international commitments, including suitable reductions where changing circumstances warrant them, are entirely appropriate. Contrary to some assertions, the United States has never been policeman to the world. Long ago, it informed the people of East Europe that it could not undertake, or even lend support to, their "liberation," much to the dismay of some of them. Its role in Africa has been quite minimal, and deliberately so. Its relations with Latin America have been important, but of a special and generally limited character. Even in the Middle East, where the United States has interests regarded as highly important, its actions have been carefully circumscribed. Only in the two regions regarded as critically important to both U.S. security and economic-political order, namely, West Europe and East Asia, has this country made sustained, major commitments. Whether mistakes in the type of commitments, or in the particular area in which commitments were made, can and should be debated, but the more this debate gets bogged down in the strawman of the global policeman image, the less productive it will be.

If isolationism is outmoded, full-fledged multilateralism is, at the very least, premature. There is every reason to enter a period of extensive but cautious experimentation with new forms of multilateral agreements in the political and military fields. Indeed, that experimentation has already commenced, and it should be encouraged. As we have noted, however, the earlier euphoria that surrounded "globalism" and various concepts of regional federation led to strong disillusionment when it was discovered that neither politically nor psychologically was the world prepared for such systems. This is an age when nationalism seems destined to remain the strongest single force in the political arena. The attacks upon it or alternatives to it, moreover, come at least as strongly from various localist, primordial attachments as they do from any willingness to accept supranational institutions. Multilateralism, therefore, can be a highly useful and even essential supplement, but it cannot represent the central ingredient of American foreign policy in Asia.

The modified alliance policy, if it is to be successful, will require much closer consultation with allies than has been characteristic of the past. As the responsibilities of various Asian states are increased, their involvement and authority must also be heightened. Further, it will be important to undergird these alliances with a growing network of private ties among the important sociopolitical components of each society. Finally, such a policy need not and should not convey an image of exclusiveness or hostility to forces external to it, including the Communist states. A part of its flexibility would consist of a willingness on the part of all parties to such alliances to explore both multilateral arrangements involving a wide range of other states and additional bilateral relations, some of them with Communist nations.

4

Regional Relations

The Pacific

Building upon the data set forth in discussing the principal societies of the Pacific-Asian region, let us now turn to the prospects within each of the regions previously defined. The Pacific region, it may be recalled, centers upon the United States, given its extensive holdings in the mid-Pacific, and upon the "island nations" extending from New Zealand and Australia in the east to those bordering the Asian continent in the west, Japan and Taiwan in the north, the Philippines and Indonesia in the south.

Only in a very loose sense can this vast expanse of ocean and land be considered a region. Perhaps even more than the other regions to which we shall refer, it is susceptible both to penetrations from without and to constant centrifugal pressures from within. Nevertheless, several features of this region have direct relevance to the Pacific-Asian area as a whole.

First, the Pacific is the center of American power. Increasingly, it will be the key to overall U.S. strategic plans and, hence, to whatever broad political-military equilibrium is achieved in the Pacific-Asian area. Our mid-Pacific bases will be the front-line defense both for the American continent and for all Pacific allies. As noted earlier, the United States will increasingly de-emphasize fixed bases in populous areas within East Asia in favor of mobile bases in the form of ships and aircraft operating primarily out of the Central Pacific.

Military Power in the Pacific. Will American military superiority in this region be challenged? The advent of Soviet military power in the Pacific has been one feature of the general growth of Soviet power throughout the entire Pacific-Asian area. In the course of the next decade, the Soviet Union is certain to expand greatly its military facilities in eastern Siberia, including its coastal bases. It is also likely to acquire new facilities in Southeast Asia via negotiations with certain governments there, notably docking-repair facilities for Soviet warships. These developments, together with the intercontinental strategic weapons systems which both superpowers now possess, signal the possibility of a Soviet effort to match American strength in the area as a whole. It should be noted, of course, that Soviet preparations are currently being developed with the China threat in mind. Nevertheless, the credibility of the American commitment to an ally in any situation involving the Soviet Union as a real or potential adversary will be put in further question.

The development of the People's Republic of China as a Pacific power is less clear, especially if we confine ourselves to the decade of the 1970s. Currently, as we have noted, China is generally concentrating upon the selective modernization of its ground and air forces and the development of a middle-range strategic weapons system, thus a system aimed primarily at such potential opponents as the Soviet Union and Japan. Would the acquisition of Taiwan affect the situation? In the longer run, the answer to such a question is almost certainly in the affirmative. The incorporation of Taiwan into the People's Republic would provide the justification, possibly the need, for a greatly expanded Chinese sea and air capacity. In addition, it would thrust China into the Pacific at a very strategic point, confronting Japan with close-in Communist presence on three of its four sides and separating it from Southeast Asia and points further to the west.

Thus, some erosion in the military superiority of the United States in this region is possible, even likely—with the Soviet Union being the principal challenger. This raises directly the question of the security programs of the other nations of the Pacific region. Is the current combination of bilateral security ties to the United States and the Southeast Asian Treaty Organization sufficient and suitable to this transitional period? If not, what should replace it?

The thrust of the Nixon Doctrine, as we have seen, is toward making every American ally responsible in greater degree for its own internal security and its primary defense against external attack. This will require that each state keep abreast of both the latest techniques for guerrilla warfare and the changing technology of conventional warfare, an area where some truly revolutionary occurrences are taking place. Defense, moreover, if it is to be effective, will have to encompass the entire field of social, economic and political policy.

At the same time, if the threat to an ally is from a nuclear power, under present circumstances, only the countervailing power of the United States may suffice. Thus, we have moved into an era in which, more than in the past, security responsibilities are divided, yet interrelated—separate, yet reciprocal. Neither the current bilateral treaties, nor SEATO with its outmoded constituency seems adequate to the tasks and challenges of the future. Logically, a much greater degree of integration among the leading non-Communist Pacific nations is warranted, whether in the form of a Pacific defense pact or some similar, if possibly less formal, arrangement. The political obstacles to such a development, however, are likely to be formidable, especially from states like Japan and Indonesia. The uncertain future status of Taiwan provides another barrier. It is likely therefore that a variety of agreements will be retained, with such coordination as is possible funnelled through American channels.

Political Systems in the Pacific Region. It is to be noted, however, that the Pacific region currently has a broad political integrity. Despite the widest cultural variations, all or almost all of the island states are committed in principle to political openness, including parliamentary institutions permitting competitive politics and a wide range of political freedoms for the citizenry. Within the region, Taiwan alone constitutes a current exception to this practice—with some restrictions existing in Indonesia and (via martial law) in the Philippines also. Even in these three societies, however, the pledge of an evolution in that direction stands in sharp contrast to the absence of any such promise by the elites of Asia's Communist states, and performance in the years ahead can be measured against the promises.

It is appropriate, however, to signal a serious and growing problem. Washington's recent reduction in the American presence in Asia and its current heavy concentration upon big power relations, combined with uncertainties about future U.S. foreign policies, have served to heighten the fears of a number of small allies—among them, South Korea, Thailand, the Philippines, and Taiwan. This in turn has led in various cases to efforts to strengthen internal controls and curb opposition—in part as preparation for a more exposed and possibly more isolated position vis-à-vis totally mobilized Communist states nearby. Previously, the substantial presence of the U.S. in Asia, together with its high credibility, enabled even states under threat and in the process of emergence to experiment with open political systems. Yet another price of any major American withdrawal might be an end to some of these experiments, as recent developments already suggest.

In the final analysis, the Asian experiments in political openness and quasi-openness are likely to be the truly decisive factors in determining whether some basic equilibrium can be achieved in Asia. No one should deny the difficulties involved in combining economic development and the quest for political openness. Nor should we forget that democracy is the most complex, most fragile political system yet devised by man, as the recent experiences of the United States itself indicate anew. Nevertheless, the experiment remains as critical to the international system of Asia as to the extent of human liberties there.

A further point deserves additional emphasis. We have already drawn attention to the growing interrelation between "domestic" and "international" politics as one of the supremely important trends of this era. This interrelation is particularly evident in open societies; and as we have suggested, it can be a telling disadvantage for them either in negotiations or in struggle with closed societies, affecting the nature and timing of concessions and, indeed, the total power of the contestants.

It thus becomes critical at this point that official relations among and between open societies be buttressed by a wide network of private relations, particularly those involving the all-important upper and middle-level opinion makers and policy-influencing groups. In this age, people-to-people diplomacy cannot remain a monopoly of the Communist world, or an instrument only of Communist-democratic relations.

Economic Relations and the Need for Community. The common political interests currently to be found among the Pacific nations are not matched in the economic sphere. Here, diversity and competition predominate, and serious problems abound. The Pacific region encompasses both "advanced" and "late developing" countries, states on the frontiers of modernity and others struggling to overcome the effects of lengthy colonial rule. Moreover, within both groups, intensive competition prevails, threatening political as well as economic relationships.

In this region, the case for multilateralism is especially powerful. A Pacific Community, established not as a substitute for but as a supplement to existing multilateral and bilateral organizations, could serve several vital needs, psychological-political as well as economic. The peoples of the Pacific, including the Americans, need a new vision and a new sense of common purpose. Unilateralism has had its day, especially in the economic arena, unless the path be marked "protection."

A Pacific Community would not seek the level of integration marking the European Community, at least not initially. Its foundations would rest upon the advanced states of the region, and it would work intently upon the full range of economic-technical relations among them, but it would also seek to develop enlightened, effective approaches to the problems of aid and assistance to developing states.

Truly bold action is needed in the field of international economics at this point. Some of that action, moreover, should take the Pacific basin as its focus. It is a grave mistake to believe that Japan, because of its level of development, can be literally removed from Asia and treated simply as if it were a part of the advanced West. This is as naive as to assume that Japan can be treated as if it were wholly Asian. In point of fact, as we have indicated, Japan belongs both to Asia and to the advanced community of nations. The place at which to accept that reality, a reality applying to certain other states of the region as well, is in the Pacific basin.

Northeast Asia

It is logical to turn next to Northeast Asia because this is a region overlapping with the Pacific region, both in area and in states. It is also the region where the largest number of major nations come into direct, intimate contact with each other. In physical terms, the United States and the U.S.S.R. are only a few miles apart at its northern extremities. Nor does one need to be reminded of the close and continuous interplay among Russia, China and Japan throughout the region. Hence, it is here that political and strategic issues frequently develop in their most acute form. It is this region, indeed, that has spawned most of the major conflicts involving Asia in the twentieth century.

The Centrality of Japan. The United States, the Soviet Union and China are all present in Northeast Asia, but Japan is at its vortex. Japan's future course of action, together with its specific relations with each of the other major powers will have an enormous influence upon trends in the region as a whole, and upon the entire Pacific-Asian area. We have suggested that in all probability, Japan will find it difficult to reach an internal consensus concerning its role in Asia, or even concerning the minimal requirements for security and the protection of its perceived interests. The quest, and the debates accompanying it, could be long and agonizing. Consequently, the danger exists that during the period when Japan is playing a relatively minimal role and being forced to negotiate largely from weakness, major policy decisions could be made and actions undertaken by China or Russia that would affect the long-range Japanese future. In some respects, and Taiwan is a case in point, such a development is already underway. Subsequently, a sharp reaction in Japan would be logical, bringing into play violent political oscillations.

How long, for instance, could Japan accept with equanimity the prospect of the Korean peninsula wholly in hostile hands, or a Taiwan fully incorporated into Peking's military-political program? At the moment, the emphasis in Sino-Japanese relations is upon negotiations and "normalization" but the future remains unclear. In the event of renewed hostility by Peking, especially if accompanied by menacing evidences of Chinese military power, would not a Japanese reaction ultimately be provoked?

As we have indicated earlier, a possibility exists that in the face of painful alternatives and a shifting balance of power, Japan might take its chances with an extremely low-posture, neutralist position, although this would require a substantial internal political change. However, given rising nationalist sentiments, and the enormous energies and capacities of the Japanese people, the most likely trend, if a more extreme response prevails, is that policy we have labelled Gaullism.

On balance, nevertheless, there is a reasonable chance that Japan will pursue a modified alliance policy in the years ahead, centering upon Japanese-American ties. Under such a policy, what possibilities exist for the region as a whole? First, overall relations among the three major states of the region excluding the United States are not likely to improve dramatically, although a series of working relationships adding up to progressive "normalization" are probable. Despite the emotional appeal of Pan-Asianism, there will be no Japanese-Chinese alliance, and indeed, the fundamental differences between these two societies today could combine with certain specific issues to evoke periodic crises. On the other hand, if the economic opportunities for Japan in China prove more extensive than is currently assumed, a new relationship might acquire stronger foundations. Emotional factors run strongly against a Japanese-Soviet alliance, as we have seen, but once again, significant economic interactions might make the ties more meaningful. In both cases, however, the range of common interests, though sufficient for accommodation, does not seem sufficient for alliance.

In its ongoing discussions with these two Communist states, it must be reiterated, Japan is currently forced to negotiate from weakness. It presents a picture of serious political division and military limitations. In negotiations, it has one positive and two negative weapons to bring to the table. On the positive side, Japan possesses great economic strength and thus the capacity to help either or both Communist giants with their developmental needs. As noted, this could be a crucial asset. However, both Moscow and Peking have consistently shown themselves wary of becoming too intimate with non-Communist states in the economic realm, and continue to emphasize economic self-sufficiency. Thus, if the strength of the Japanese economy is to be a truly potent weapon, basic changes in Communist attitudes and policies will have to occur.

The negative weapons may be at least equally effective. Japan can employ the classic technique of the small state confronted with major powers, that of playing one against the other. Even if this technique is not employed actively, it comes into operation automatically, as recent Soviet overtures toward Japan indicate so clearly. The other negative weapon is a more uncertain one, that of threatening to accelerate Japanese military capacities, conventional or nuclear. Under present conditions such a threat would be more likely to concern China than the Soviet Union, although neither would be happy with a nuclear Japan.

In any case, we can anticipate carefully bargained, relatively nongenerous agreements between Japan and the major Communist states, with each party fully aware of the other's strengths and weaknesses. Such a situation, however, might be conducive to a general balancing of the major forces in this region. The American-Japanese alliance, with its increased flexibility and the added element of Japanese independence, will endure but will seem less threatening to Peking and Moscow. In certain respects, indeed, it may even seem an advantage— particularly if it serves to forestall the Japanese development of nuclear weapons. Meanwhile, both the Soviet Union and China will be served if Japan achieves less than an alliance with the other. On the other hand, some degree of normalization of relations with both would encourage a lowering of tensions and the peaceful settlement of at least some disputes.

The Korean Scene. To achieve this set of relations among the major powers of Northeast Asia with these results, the two critical problems to which we earlier referred will have to be resolved in a fashion relatively acceptable to all parties. A unified, Communist Korea would represent an unacceptable risk to Japan—if not immediately, at least over time. A unified, non-Communist Korea cannot be accepted by China, especially given the importance of its Manchurian industrial complex. Peace and stability in Northeast Asia thus hinge, for the time being, upon the acceptance by all of the major powers of a divided Korea, painful although this is to the Korean people. Notwithstanding certain recent dramatic developments in South-North Korean relations, to suggest the establishment of a unified, neutralized Korea at this point in history is no more realistic, given the nature of the internal and external forces involved, than to propose the establishment of a unified neutralized Germany.

Would a four-power guarantee of the sovereignty and integrity of the two Koreas pending their *peaceful* unification provide a desirable, or acceptable, substitute for the present bilateral security treaties which both Koreas have with their respective guarantors? The Communists have made it clear that they favor some such development, primarily to remove American power from the scene and to ensure that Japanese power shall not replace it. The critical question, however, is as yet unanswered. How would such a guarantee be enforced, if violated? As long as Kim Il-sŏng lives, at least, the North Korean commitment to "liberate" the South is certain to stand, although Kim is now dedicated to the tactics of Vietnam, post-1960, not Korea-1950. Recent pledges do not basically alter long-range Korean Communist goals. Will anything other than a firm American commitment suffice to prevent North Korean adventurism? Until these questions can be satisfactorily answered, it is not logical to experiment with the security of South Korea via a loose form of multilateralism. To do so, indeed, would jeopardize relations among all of the major states of the region.

90

The Taiwan Issue. The Taiwan issue is equally troublesome. Here, the People's Republic of China has scored certain major political gains in the recent past. There can be no doubt that the Shanghai Communique of 1972 signed by Nixon and Chou En-lai represented a significant victory for Peking on the Taiwan question, at least from a psychological-political standpoint. Instead of asserting that the two governments on both sides of the Taiwan Straits averred that China and Taiwan were one, which would have been a simple statement of fact, the communique read that "all of the people" on both sides of the straits so insisted, making it a false statement and hence a significant American concession. Even earlier, however, the United States seemed to send out signals that Taiwan was expendable, up to a point at least, when Henry Kissinger undertook a second trip to Peking precisely at the time when the issue of Chinese representation was before the United Nations.

Subsequent official reiterations of support for U.S. treaty commitments with Taiwan have not materially changed the situation. American policy rests upon the assumption that the status quo in Taiwan can be maintained for the near future at least, with Peking prepared to wait for some natural evolution in its direction. Any incorporation of Taiwan into the mainland will supposedly take place in stages, moreover, with substantial autonomy for the island and its people in the first phases. But if these assumptions prove incorrect, as is very possible, Taiwan could become an explosive issue involving all of the major powers of the area.

There is little indication that negotiations between the Nationalists on Taiwan and the Communists on the mainland can succeed, given the historic relations between the two groups and the events that have occurred on the mainland in the past twenty years. In politics, one can never rule out a deal, but the likelihood in this instance does not seem high. A second stage will then be reached, one in which the Communists will apply increasing economic and political pressure against Taiwan, with the major targets being Japan and the United States. In the past, Peking has applied considerable pressure in an effort to curb Japanese trade and investment with Taiwan. However, it appears willing at this point for Japanese economic relations with Taiwan to continue, in part because of the political and legal concessions obtained through the joint communique of September 29, 1972 and in part because of its determination to block the further advances of Soviet containment policies. Efforts to discourage American investment will probably take a different form, with an emphasis upon the risks involved. The objective will be economic strangulation unless an accommodation is reached. Meanwhile, political activities will be stepped up. Already, Taiwanese students in both Japan and the United States are targets for Peking's overtures, and such activities will be accelerated. Ultimately, if some agreement upon annexation has not been achieved, there will be an effort to launch an underground movement in Taiwan itself.

Thus, Peking's tactics will consist of cumulative economic, political and psychological pressure rather than the use of overt military force. It is always possible, we reiterate, that at some point, a governing elite in Taiwan will agree to accept Communist control. Such an agreement would presumably pledge initial autonomy for the island, and this has been seized upon by some observers as the ideal solution. Autonomy, however, has had a very special meaning to the Chinese Communists —as the three cases of the Inner-Mongolian Autonomous Region, the Kwangsi Autonomous Region, and Tibet illustrate—and it is virtually impossible to conceive of them allowing true autonomy for any considerable period of time. In the three other instances, the Communist party has quickly assumed a dominant, if partially concealed role, and political cadres have immediately begun the undermining of the existing order. To approach the problem in any other fashion would be to violate all Communist precepts and experience. At best, autonomy would be a fig leaf, fragile and temporary.

Is it conceivable, however, that under the conditions outlined above, Taiwan will stand still, frozen in institutional and political terms? This seems highly unlikely. On the one hand, as we have suggested, a Communist campaign directed at securing allegiance from the Taiwanese, and particularly from the youth, will surely be mounted. The stress will be more upon nationalism than upon communism in all probability, with an appeal to join a new, powerful China. What success such a campaign will have, it is difficult to say. In the past, apart from the mainland refugees, the people of Taiwan have had no particular commitment to the mainland, and it has generally been acknowledged that if they could have a free choice, they would choose independence. Will an appeal to Chinese nationalism—and the absence of clear-cut alternatives—change that situation?

Meanwhile, it can be assumed that an institutional evolution may take place on Taiwan. For twenty years, that island has been a de facto state entirely separate from the People's Republic of China and growing apart from it at an accelerated rate—in economy, culture, and way of life. It is unlikely, at least at this point, that the Taiwanese independence movement could flourish in its old forms. Its leadership is too weak and divided, its organization too shallow. However, independence can take many forms, including that of gradual evolution toward separate *and* representative political institutions. Already, the fiction that Taiwan is China has been largely abandoned and, sooner or later, this will find increased expression politically, as the ruling party turns outward to the Taiwanese people for support. The first stages of such a development, indeed, are already underway.

The alternative to accommodation between China and Taiwan is thus not merely the status quo, but an accelerating evolution (possibly accompanied by some element of turmoil) on Taiwan, with political as well as economic institutions undergoing change. In such an eventuality, what will be the attitude and policy of the major powers of the region? Japan, has now come exceedingly close to a formal acceptance of the principle that Taiwan is a province of China. But as noted earlier, the prospect of a Peking-controlled Taiwan directly south of Japan is not an attractive one to many Japanese. The Tanaka government paid most of the price Peking demanded for normalization, but Japan would not be unhappy if Taiwan continued to exist as an independent state.

If Taiwan evolved toward an independent status institutionally, would American treaty obligations be maintained? And what would be the American reaction should Taiwan at some point seek international recognition as an entity separate from China? The United States appears to hope that it will not have to face these questions, and that the Taiwan issue can be set on the shelf for a period, with a "satisfactory" solution ultimately forthcoming. We are in a new "let the dust settle" period.

Meanwhile, it is not entirely clear that the Soviet Union really wants China to incorporate Taiwan, thereby gaining a Pacific status that would require additional air and sea power and affecting at least potentially the Soviet position in Siberian and western Pacific waters. On occasion, Soviet diplomats have talked privately in ambiguous terms after the future of Taiwan, indicating some interest in keeping the issue open.

Whatever the trends with respect to the Korean and Taiwan issues, these are both problems having a direct bearing upon relations among the major powers of the Northeast Asian region. Such relations, in turn, will have a decisive impact upon both the overall balance of power in the Pacific-Asian area and the general level of harmony or friction marking developments in the 1970s. The prospects for the big issues— peaceful coexistence and weapons control—hinge upon developments here, making this region the key to the Pacific-Asian future from a political and strategic standpoint. And most indications point to a slow, often painful period of negotiations—without war, but without massive, decisive breakthroughs either.

The Continental Center

The twenty-fifth century historian, looking back on this era, will surely record the Sino-Soviet cleavage as one of the truly significant political events of the twentieth century. At the outset of the 1950s, an alliance had seemingly bound together for the indefinite future two nations capable of dominating the Eurasian continent. In population alone, nearly a billion people were involved, with great energy and vast resources at their disposal. Profound repercussions from this alliance were threatened upon all of the small states on its peripheries. Yet in less than a decade, Russia and China had resumed that stance of mutual suspicion and hostility more in keeping with their historic relations.

Sino-Soviet Confrontation. Sino-Soviet relations not only dominate Asia's continental center; they are the exclusive relations of this region, all else being trivial. Therein lies one of the central problems for the two nations. Few potential buffer states exist in this region that can serve to moderate the close-in presence of these two major societies. On the contrary, the natural buffer zones of the past have been eroded. Formerly, de facto Russia and China tapered off as one moved toward the center of the Asian land mass, with a congeries of tribal peoples, loosely related and loosely governed, moving about over inner Asia. Today, however, both the U.S.S.R. and the People's Republic of China have acted resolutely to fill this vacuum, moving their populations and their power to the frontiers, bringing tribal peoples under strict control, and thereby facing each other directly and in close proximity.

94

In the whole of inner Asia, there are only two independent states. One of these, Afghanistan, is not situated geographically to play the role of a true buffer state, although it has important borders with Russia and some rather minor borders with China. The other, Outer Mongolia, is a client state, not a buffer state, primarily because of its great and legitimate fear of being absorbed by China. The fact that its population is only one million, and that there are more Mongols within China than in the Mongolian People's Republic explains the reasons for Mongolia's status.

Given this situation, it is natural that the complex issues which have emerged to disrupt relations between China and Russia would ultimately come to focus on questions of basic security and would find their concrete expression in two armed camps facing each other on the frontier. It is also natural that both states would gravitate toward balance of power politics, but with their concept of balance made somewhat more complex by the necessity to vie for a position in the international "revolutionary" world as well as in the world of existing states.

The cleavage between China and Russia has impelled both nations to move rapidly from simple to complex relations with the external world. This fact alone makes the reestablishment of the Sino-Soviet alliance in its earlier, "pure" form difficult to envisage. It must be reiterated, however, that dramatic shifts, "favorable" or "unfavorable," cannot be ruled out in this unique situation.

As noted earlier, one of the reasons for the bitterness and intractability of the Sino-Soviet dispute has been the degree to which each side has been involved, both consciously and unconsciously, in the internal politics of the other. The first issues made this inevitable. They were nationalist issues of relative power and authority, coupled with pragmatic issues involving the merits of different developmental strategies. Positions once taken, however, had to be justified in ideological terms. Thus, the legitimacy of each elite had to be challenged and its right to rule questioned. This meant deep involvement in each side's domestic politics. It became easy, moreover, in the case of China, for the "Maoists" to attack opponents by labelling them "pro-Khrushchevite."

Few, if any, Chinese Communist leaders of recent times can be labelled staunchly "pro-Russian." It is likely, however, that a number of them regarded the deep split as not in China's interest. Despite the importance, one might even say inevitability, of the substantive issues that emerged between the two nations, moreover, the evidence indicates that the human element in the dispute has not been insignificant.[29] Thus, it is possible, as the current Russian leaders hope, that changes in top Chinese (or Soviet) leadership might produce a reversal of recent trends. There is a difference, however, between normalization, even an accelerated movement toward normalization, and a restored alliance. Given the events of the past decade, the latter prospect seems dim.

Thus, it is wise to assume that the relationship between the Soviet Union and China will continue to be more competitive than cooperative, both in the Pacific-Asian area and in the global scene.

The Status of the Small States. This situation offers hope for various small countries in the shadow of Soviet or Chinese power, irrespective of the political banners which they fly. Ideally, both Russia and China desire spheres of influence and, prior to the split between them, that seemed an inevitable development, with Russia firmly in control of Europe or at least Eastern Europe, and China ascendant in Asia or at least continental Asia. Now, however, the Soviet Union has made it clear that it is prepared to challenge Chinese hegemony in such a region as Southeast Asia, separately from whatever challenge the United States or other nations may issue. The Chinese have responded appropriately in East Europe.

Under these circumstances, nonalignment and a greater degree of independence may be possible for states previously destined to be clients or satellites of one or the other of the Communist giants. Such a development, indeed, is the only available substitute for the buffer state system that is not physically possible. Thus for Asia as for Europe, the true significance of the Sino-Soviet cleavage lies in the fact that it permits a much more differentiated world, with a great deal more leverage for small states, both individually and in regional groupings.

One should not exaggerate these opportunities. Small neighboring states still must determine the tolerance level of the Russians and the Chinese—to discern precisely what degree of independence is acceptable, what nonalignment means to Moscow and Peking and, most importantly, how to time and measure those shifts within a nonaligned, inde-

---

[29] The polemics published on the Sino-Soviet dispute by both major parties reveal not merely differences over important substantive issues, but Chinese bitterness as a result of Khrushchev's relatively brusk diplomatic manners and Soviet resentment in turn of Mao's "imperious, xenophobic" nature.

pendent policy that changing circumstances require. Clearly, the problem of a North Korea which has boundaries with both major Communist states will be different from that of a North Vietnam which borders China but is separated from the Soviet Union by a huge distance. Nor will the problem be the same for various non-Communist states, also possessing different geographic, political and socioeconomic characteristics.

Nevertheless, as long as the Soviet Union and China regard each other as primary opponents and feel the need to focus extensive military attention upon the continental center, greater diversity will be possible on the peripheries of the Sino-Soviet orbit. Other Communist states and parties, however, will suffer because of the centrifugal tendencies which the Soviet-Chinese rift produces within their own ranks. Correspondingly, Russian and Chinese spheres of influence will continue to be porous, as both parties attempt to secure a favorable overall balance of power.

Southeast Asia

Our attention has already been directed toward Southeast Asia because it is one of the regions most critically affected by the Sino-Soviet cleavage. It seems clear that no simple formula is likely to succeed in bringing stability or economic growth to this area. "Neutralization" has been a recurrent theme and, as a goal, it has considerable merit. Each of the major Pacific-Asian powers wants access to this vitally important region, with its two hundred and fifty million people and its rich natural resources. Domination of the region by a single power, moreover, would have a strongly adverse effect upon any broader political-military equilibrium in the Pacific-Asian area.

This is a region, however, as rich in problems as it is in resources. In most of the Southeast Asian "states," subcultures coexist uneasily within political boundaries newly established and partly artificial. National consciousness tends to be low, politics volatile and personalized. The urban-rural gap is growing, as is the distance between the intellectual-professional classes and the peasant. Political institutions and goals differ widely throughout the region, as do living standards and rates of growth. Two terms sum up existing conditions with reasonable fairness: diversity and instability. Southeast Asia remains a vacuum of power and a region where the status quo is unacceptable to many despite some signs of growth in recent years.

Consequently, external intervention in this region has been substantial, not by one major power but by all. The United States sought in some measure to fill the vacuum left by the rapidly departing European powers—partly to prevent China, or some united front involving China and Indonesia, from exercising overweening influence throughout the region. Subsequently, the Soviet Union has rapidly expanded its influence in the region, also in an effort to contain China, but with its own economic and political interests in mind as well—and without any wish to see American influence entrenched there. Japan, meantime, has reconstructed its co-prosperity sphere in Southeast Asia without the heavy political and military overtones of the pre-World War II version.

Finally, China's presence in Southeast Asia has been felt in a variety of ways: in its drive for a broad political united front encompassing Communists and neutralists, a drive now confined largely to Indochina, via sponsorship of the Alliance of Indochinese Peoples; in its sometimes covert, sometimes overt, support of Communist movements that are out of power and seeking to overthrow existing governments; in its continuing contacts with the overseas Chinese communities of the area; and finally, in its overtures for official relations with some, but not all, of the existing non-Communist governments of the region. Nowhere in the world has the People's Republic of China mixed and varied the state-to-state, people-to-people, and comrade-to-comrade components of its foreign policy in a more fascinating manner than in Southeast Asia. At the same time, there is increasing evidence to suggest that with the principal Communist state of the region, North Vietnam, China's relations currently represent a complex admixture of cooperation and competition.

Given all of the facts, this region represents a critical test case for the principles of peaceful coexistence and the effectiveness of negotiations in place of confrontation. Can the complex problems engendering conflict be contained if not solved via the route of negotiations? If this is to occur, the following principles will probably have to be established:

1. The existence of de facto states will ultimately have to be recognized—with the proviso that strictly internal conflicts warrant a

hands-off policy by all other states and that changes attempted by external sources, either through armed force or internal subversion, constitute aggression.

2. The major powers must agree to remove their military presence from the area and to limit military assistance in the form of arms and training to recognized governments and to specified, mutually agreed amounts.

3. An international commission which includes the major powers should be established to maintain constant liaison and to consider complaints relating to the activities of states external to the region.

4. Joint economic aid and development programs should be undertaken through the World Bank, the International Monetary Fund, the Asian Development Bank, and similar organizations, with the hope of participation and cooperation of the Communist states.

5. Bilateral military agreements should be replaced by a multilateral guarantee on the part of the major powers. This should be coupled with the creation of a regional commission composed strictly of the states of the area, whose primary purpose would be to consider security violations perpetrated by indigenous states or parties.

6. Those indigenous states so inclined should be permitted to form a regional defense group which would come to the aid of any member attacked by external forces, and this group would also cooperate in border patrol activities.

Southeast Asia is unique. Reflecting that fact, the above proposals differ from those that would be appropriate at this point in other regions of the Pacific-Asian area. The choice here is essentially between the risks of multilateralism combined with a strengthened indigenous regionalism and the risks of a polarized region comprised of competing spheres of influence subject to challenge and further confrontation.

If multilateralism can succeed in this region, it will only be because the interests of the major powers are carefully balanced and have certain limits as well as certain potentials for compatibility. In essence, if each of the major states outside the region finds that crisis management (rather than escalation), limited involvement, and mutual access are in its interest, and if the capacities of the region itself to handle internal problems can be raised, some emergence from the anarchic past may be conceivable.

The future of South Asia, as suggested earlier, hinges strongly upon the internal stability and growth potential of India, now clearly the dominant nation of the region. Various recent developments have occurred to make the Congress party—and the central government—look stronger at this point than at any time since Indian independence. The major military victory over Pakistan produced a surge of nationalist pride, greatly benefiting the ruling party and its leader. Mrs. Gandhi, moreover, has proven to be a far more skillful political manipulator than her opponents realized. Finally, the failure of left Communist rule in West Bengal and the deep, internecine warfare within the left in this region have enabled the Congress to regain control in decisive fashion.

As in the case of China, however, long-range predictions concerning internal political trends in India are hazardous. Congress is as much a movement as it is a party. Internal fissures have been a constant feature of its history, and there is little reason to believe that this problem will be solved quickly or easily. Moreover, while the so-called "right" in Indian politics seems to have been vanquished for the foreseeable future, that is far from the case with portions of the "left," notably the Communist party of India—Marxist (CPI-M), notwithstanding its recent setbacks. Mrs. Gandhi's shift to the left, including her internal alliance with the CPI (the "right-wing" Communist party of India, Moscow-aligned) undoubtedly helped to further split Indian Communists and put the left off balance. But in ousting the left Communists from leadership in West Bengal, Congress was unable to rely upon parliamentary means alone. Extra-parliamentary actions, including the use of naked force, were involved. Let it quickly be stated that the CPI-M and its further left opponents, the Naxalites, had pioneered in such tactics. Nevertheless, the duration of Congress's new mandate remains uncertain, particularly since its capacity to keep that mandate strong by effective actions has only begun to be tested. Democracy has one corruptive, potentially disastrous effect that could be particularly acute in a society like India's: it tends to yield power to those who promise the most in the way of benefits and demand the least in the way of sacrifice. Thus expectations are raised without being fulfilled, and highly unrealistic programs, particularly in the economic realm, are advanced because politicians find them attractive as short-range expediencies—even necessities. Can Congress escape the implications of this democratic "law"?

Meanwhile, it is likely that the international relations of the region have recently assumed a pattern that will prevail for some time. The new Soviet-Indian alliance generally accords with both internal and external trends. At home, the political trend within the Congress party continues to be leftward, including an ever stronger reliance upon a statist approach to economic development. In a mixed economy where the private sector was vigorous and being given encouragement, a rising, dynamic interaction with a nation like Japan might be expected. Current Indian economic trends seem to diminish any such possibilities. Abroad, China remains a perceived threat to both India and the U.S.S.R., with the new alliance being essentially a response to this fact.

The very existence of the new ties, moreover, is likely to exacerbate Sino-Indian difficulties. At present, the People's Republic of China has no interest in seeking a rapprochement with India. It regards Indian policy as a part of the broader Soviet design to contain Peking. But why, many Indians ask, does not China make a concerted effort to woo India and thus interfere with the Soviet-Indian alliance? The answers would appear to be these: China does not fear India as a threatening source of independent power. Thus, in comparison with Japan and Northeast Asia, India and South Asia have a much lower priority. Moreover, since India is seen essentially as an appendage to the Soviet threat, China continues to see merit in maintaining a countervailing set of ties centering upon Pakistan and—potentially at least—other states of the region.

The Chinese quest for a balance of power in South Asia has been badly damaged, to be sure, by the developments of 1971-1972. It is important to emphasize, however, that the Chinese, seeing no urgency in this particular situation, are prepared to accept certain immediate losses and wait for more favorable trends. They recognize that the Bhutto government in Pakistan, moving away from its old SEATO and CENTO ties centering upon the United States, may well come ever closer to Peking. They are also aware of the fact that many of the small states in South Asia, unhappy over the omnipresence of Indian power, would not object to a more meaningful political-military equilibrium, enabling them to exercise greater independence of action. They are also

101

confident that political trends within the new state of Bangladesh will turn in their direction at some point. Thus, China remains unworried about India on the one hand, and unreconciled to the new order in South Asia on the other. It can be expected to exploit favorable political developments, when and if these occur. Its methods will not be those of overt military intervention, but of political-military involvement via "progressive" and "liberation" forces.

For the near future at least, a Soviet-Indian alliance will confront a Chinese-Pakistan entente, with some small states of the region aligned, others not. In this, an element of equilibrium theory persists, despite the newly achieved Indian dominance of the subcontinent. The United States, under these circumstances, is likely to hold its commitments in South Asia to a relatively low level. An element of "neutralism" is also likely to be present in its policies, especially for the duration of the "leftist" trend in India and the growing fluidity of politics in Pakistan. Under present conditions, there are few incentives for heavy American involvement in South Asia, and many risks. This region in general and India in particular are not and cannot be high on the American foreign policy priority list, for reasons previously set forth. America's primary concerns must be with the two crucial triangles, U.S.-U.S.S.R.-China and U.S.-Japan-West Europe. These relations, together with the volatile Middle Eastern situation will command the highest priorities. It is true that some of the historic issues dividing the United States and India may have been resolved by events. For example, to aim at a political-military equilibrium between Pakistan and India, as did classic American policy, is unrealistic at this point unless Chinese and Russian forces are factored into the equation. Even then, this objective seems a dubious one for American policy. It might be assumed also that the elements of personal animosity against the United States, noticeably strong in both Nehru and his daughter, Mrs. Gandhi, and having their counterpart in anti-Indian attitudes within certain American policy-making circles, might fade as relations shift to a different basis and expectations on both sides become less intense. The need for an end to the old aid-based relationship—and to over-emphasis upon such sentimental themes as "the two largest democracies of the world"—has long been clear to realists on both sides. From a low profile and minimal involvement, a new relationship may be possible.

The elements of uncertainty and contradiction within the South Asian scene should not be minimized. As we have noted, the probabilities lie with a continuance of the international order now prevailing. India, however, entered its alliance with the Soviet Union with certain qualms. Recent developments, moreover, particularly the events in the Middle East, have raised the first questions about Soviet credibility in the minds of prominent Indians previously favorable or resigned to the alliance. Some quiet rethinking, including the reexamination of other broad alternatives has commenced in the higher levels of Indian official-dom. From the Soviet standpoint also, the recent heavy commitments to the subcontinent may eventually become counterproductive. Extensive involvement in the problems of this region, economic and political, is likely to be costly and to yield uncertain results. Moreover, there remain huge cultural barriers between the new allies, barriers not easily removed.

Nevertheless, India is not nonaligned today, and the process leading to alliance was begun long ago. As has been noted, the Nehru era ended disastrously for India in terms of its previously held view of its interests and status in the world. A fundamental reordering of foreign policies has followed, although lip-service continues to be paid to such historic phrases as nonalignment. It can be argued, moreover, that under prevailing circumstances, the alliance with the Soviet Union serves Indian national interests, especially if one accepts the ideological and political perspectives of the leftist Congress leaders. It can also be asserted that in this "multipolar" era, alliances need not be tightly knit, exclusive relationships, a critical point which we shall explore shortly.

A second question involving South Asia concerns the degree to which this region can retain or create an integrity of its own and exist relatively aloof from broader international currents. As we have seen, South Asia has enjoyed great natural boundaries in the north, effectively separating it for long periods of time from close involvement with the central Eurasian continent, or Northeast Asia. Contacts with Southeast Asia—and with Asia Minor—were generally easier to sustain. Even today, the Himalayas constitute a formidable barrier. But all available signs suggest that modern communications and weaponry, together with the universalization of certain values, lessen the separateness and integrity that once existed.

In any case, however, trends within India itself are likely to determine the degree of stability or instability for South Asia as a whole for the near future. This is now a region possessing one dominant indigenous force. The international relations within the region and, to a considerable extent, between the region and others will depend upon India's capacities to stabilize its newly found regional role while at the same time, advancing domestic order and economic growth.

5

An Overview

Understandably, those who study our international system seek terms that can convey its essence in the most efficient, succinct manner. Thus, at one point, "bipolarity" enjoyed wide usage. Today, the "in" word is "multipolarity." Both of these terms have had their utility, but each, once enthroned, has exercised a degree of tyranny, threatening to drive more complex truths underground.

Bipolarism and Its Limits. When, for example, did "bipolarity" begin and end? Even to pose this question is to introduce some of the complexities that have attended the international scene since 1945. Immediately after World War II there was only one superpower, namely, the United States. It was the only major, modern nation that had survived that war with minimal damage and with greatly augmented military, political and economic power. It alone possessed nuclear weapons, together with massive conventional forces, virtually intact. American industries, wholly undamaged, had a productive capacity unmatched elsewhere in the world. Not least important, the United States enjoyed unprecedented political stability. Its people were as unified, and their morale as high, as at any time in American history. In sum, all of the ingredients of power were present in remarkably full measure.

In retrospect, it was natural that the United States should quickly assume broad international responsibilities, having made a radical break with isolationism when it entered the war. The Soviet Union, to be sure, also had military power, as well as the will to use that power, especially in Europe. There can be no real comparison, however, between its total power and that of the United States in the first decade after

World War II. Nor can the scope of their commitments be equated. The U.S.S.R., with European Russia devastated by the war, took a full seven years to regain the productive levels of the prewar era. These were miserable years for the Soviet citizen. Victory in the war, however, together with severe penalties for all types of dissidence, sufficed to provide political unity. Moreover, Soviet armies remained powerful, and a concerted effort to acquire nuclear weapons was begun.

Nevertheless, in this period, the Soviet Union was a regional, not a global, power. Its power extended primarily into Eastern Europe, the region of its most vital international interests. The only other region of substantial commitment was at the other end of the Eurasian continent (and Soviet boundaries) in North Korea and China—where wartime and postwar developments had placed inescapable requirements upon the Russians. The deep imbalance of American and Soviet power during this period is fully revealed in Soviet tactics. When a series of issues brought the United States and the Soviet Union into serious confrontation, Stalin carefully avoided direct conflict. Instead, he called upon comrades everywhere to use *their* power via guerrilla warfare and any other available technique, including conventional war, to stop American "imperialism." The North Koreans and the Chinese Communists were to pay a heavy price for their response to this appeal, while Soviet power continued to gain ground.

By the mid- and late-1950s, the picture became more complex. The Soviet Union had acquired nuclear weapons and, while its strength in this field was far from that of the United States, it now possessed what some regarded as a "credible nuclear deterrent." Domestic Soviet economic and political policies achieved mixed results, but on balance they probably were successful enough to enhance Soviet power. Economic development accelerated, albeit unevenly, with agriculture remaining a serious bottleneck. After the death of Stalin, political conditions improved for the average Soviet citizen, but the de-Stalinization campaign created serious problems of Soviet credibility among overseas comrades. Who could be certain, in the light of this campaign, that any given Soviet line would be a firm, relatively permanent one? Thus, in contradictory fashion, Soviet power was subjected to a certain erosion within the Communist world, even as that power—measured in sheer military and economic terms—rapidly advanced. When the first test came, however, Russian power was sufficient to uphold the status quo in Eastern Europe against a series of challenges stemming from internal upheavals. The United States elected not to risk a major war on behalf of East Europe, its earlier propaganda for "liberation" notwithstanding.

Bipolarism had its greatest validity in this period. To its initial Eurasian commitments, the Soviet Union selectively added others, as various opportunities presented themselves in the Middle East, Africa, and even the Caribbean (Cuba). The United States, meanwhile, carrying forward its containment policy with respect to both the Soviet Union and China, was reaching the zenith of its international commitments via a complex alliance-and-aid structure encompassing many states. The ideological component within international relations tended to be relatively high. Correspondingly, communications between the Communist and Western blocs were generally polemical and limited. Alliances thus assumed an intense, all-encompassing, exclusivist character. In these senses, polarization was abetted, with the two poles being Washington and Moscow.

In many respects however, bipolarism was more a symbol of the broad thrust of Soviet-American relations than an accurate depiction of the world as it actually existed—even at the height of the so-called bipolar period. In the first place, a number of natural and self-imposed limitations existed with respect to the commitments and involvements of the two superpowers. The thesis that the United States played the role of global policeman is one of those distortions useful in political infighting, but factually deficient. The United States, for very good reasons, always placed its first priorities on West Europe and East Asia. Its commitments in the Middle East were significant, but generally limited. Those in Latin America (excluding the neighboring Caribbean) were also limited, and special in character, while commitments in Africa were relatively minimal. For the Soviet Union, East Europe retained first priority, with the Middle East gradually assuming a role of second importance. Aside from certain special (and highly important) commitments such as those to China, North Korea, and Cuba, Soviet allocations of military or economic resources elsewhere were limited. The concept—later propagated assiduously by Peking—that the United States and the Soviet Union had divided the world between them in papal fashion, was no more correct than subsequent Soviet assertions that Washington and Peking were engaged in a conspiracy to handle Asian problems in accordance with their mutual interests. Whatever mistakes each may have made in assessing its capacities or interests, both the United States and the Soviet Union retained a sense of priorities throughout the so-called bipolar period. As a result, certain regions were accorded minimal importance, some were excluded altogether and others were singled out for special treatment.

It was in this period, moreover, that nonalignment and neutralism had their finest hours, another comment upon the limits of bipolarism. Only a few nations were accorded a nonaligned status by mutual Soviet-American agreement, most of them serving as buffer states. Given the character of alliances in the cold war period, however, and the strong nationalist drives motivating the new states, it was natural that many "emerging" nations sought to remain outside the alliance structure, hoping in some cases to avail themselves of the resources of both superpowers without being beholden to either. Given this goal and the prevailing ideological fashions, it was also natural that many new states sought to take a neutralist political stance, portraying themselves as standing between the "capitalist" and "Communist" worlds.

This "third world" was always less united, less neutral, and less important in international politics than its self-proclaimed spokesmen were prepared to admit. Nevertheless, neutralism was a widely heralded position in the bipolar period, evidence once again of the risks involved in applying all-encompassing labels to the global scene.

Finally, bipolarism should not be used to connote an equal balance of power, however power be defined at this point. The Soviet Union and the Communist bloc which it led had achieved a tenable defensive position. The importance of this is not to be minimized. It would certainly not be accurate, however, to regard the military, economic or political capacities of the two contending forces as approximately equal. On the contrary, the bipolar period was dominated by the superior power of the so-called Western bloc led by the United States. In military terms, as we have noted, the Soviet Union has only approached parity with the United States in the recent past, after the onset of "multipolarism." In economic terms as well, the "advanced" world as a unit (the United States, Western Europe and Japan) far outdistanced the "socialist" world (the U.S.S.R., East Europe and other Communist states) in the bipolar period. Even in psychological political terms, trends with respect to stability, national will, and governmental credibility were more favorable to the Western bloc during this period than at a later point. These facts were appreciated by the Soviet Union even if they were not always accepted by some of its more zealous allies.

When did bipolarism end? Presumably, its end was signalled by the advent of two seemingly contradictory developments: the failure of the Sino-Soviet alliance and the success of the American-sponsored rehabilitation of West Europe and Japan. Unquestionably, these two developments did much to change the politics of the late twentieth century world. The widening cleavage between Russia and China disrupted the unity of the Communist world at every level and on nearly every issue. Now, international relations *within* the Communist world traverse the same range from alliance, through neutrality, to enmity as has historically been the condition of Western international relations. Meanwhile, the revitalization of West Europe and Japan provided the basis for increasing self-assertion and more independent initiatives from these states.

Multipolarism—Thrust of the Future? Multipolarism, however, is at best a highly imprecise description of the current international order, whether the discussion be confined to the Pacific-Asian area or broadened to include the world at large. Which states represent the principal poles of our multipolar world? It has been customary in recent times to speak of five major "powers," meaning the United States, the Soviet Union, the People's Republic of China, Japan and the West European community. Our earlier analysis, however, should have made it clear that to group these five powers together in any undifferentiated fashion is to use the concept of power in diverse, potentially incompatible ways.

In strictly military terms, the gap between the United States and the Soviet Union on the one hand and any other nation or conceivable alliance of nations on the other has widened, not narrowed, during the past decade. As has been noted, the most significant military development during that period has been the narrowing of the gap *between* Russia and America. One can, of course, point to certain countervailing currents. First, there is the general proliferation of military power throughout the world, partly as a result of American and Soviet military assistance. Thus, even if no single nation actually competes with the U.S. or the U.S.S.R. militarily, nonetheless the global scene is less susceptible to manipulation by a single major actor, even by a superpower, than was the case at an earlier point. Further, inhibitions restraining the superpowers from using total power against a third party have grown stronger with the passage of time and events. This is particularly true of any contemplated use of nuclear weapons, but it applies in the arena of "conventional" warfare as well. We are dealing here with a murky subject, replete with fuzzy political and psychological factors, but it remains true to say that both the United States and the Soviet Union have probably accepted the principle that, in most conflict situations, they will settle for the use of only a portion of their military power, even if the result is something less than total victory. At least insofar as the United States is concerned, the concept of limited war has been an accepted, if highly debated, axiom of American foreign policy for more than two decades.

With respect to limited war, the Soviet Union has not really been put to the test as yet. That in itself may be highly significant. Russia has not been loathe to employ military power in recent years as one weapon for pursuing its conceived national interests, whether in the form of overt use (Czechoslovakia), threat (China), or for utilization by others (North Vietnam, the Arab states). Indeed, as has been emphasized, the early phases of the multipolar era have witnessed a considerable expansion of Soviet commitments, many of them resting upon military power—even as the United States has been involved in some degree of contraction. By the same token, the new Soviet commitments, like the old American ones, have brought various forms of strain and tension to the donor.

Is the effective reach of Soviet (American) military power less today than in the bipolar period? If the answer is yes, it must be more because of increased psychological and political restraints against the total use of such power than because of truly effective military counterweights. Since such restraints—even if they are present in the case of both superpowers—necessarily affect each in different degree and are likely to vary with the precise issues and adversaries to be faced, any sweeping unequivocal answers are suspect. In any case, however, there is clearly no equality of military strength among the five major powers noted above. As has been indicated, China is on its way to achieving significant military power, from all indications, and even now must be considered a formidable adversary by all of the states on its borders except the Soviet Union. However, it will not attain military parity with either the United States or Russia in the conceivable future. And such an eventuality seems even less likely in the case of Japan or West Europe—given current and predictable political-military trends.

This does not necessarily mean that these lesser military powers cannot develop an effective defense, combining available military, political and economic instrumentalities. In conflict-of-interest situations, indeed, very considerable bargaining leverage or offensive capacity may be available to them, even when one of the superpowers is the primary adversary. In general terms, these states—and others—can use the continuing diversity of American and Soviet interests, or of Soviet and Chinese interests, to their advantage. Politics in a multipolar period thus normally affords a more intricate set of political responses.

As we have seen, however, neutralism as Nehru envisaged it has very limited possibilities in a multipolar period. In such a world, there are no opposite extremities, no two polar points against which to take a centrist position. Only if one practices isolation in a relatively extreme sense and proscribes all but the most minimal relations with the major societies is neutralism easy to envisage. Even then, as the case of Burma shows, it may not be reciprocated in like manner by the parties toward which it is directed. Nonalignment also has become more difficult, at least for the major societies. In a multipolar period, the nonaligned state may find itself bereft of any substantive support in time of crisis. Issues and events, moreover, have conspired to tilt the political positions of most of the smaller states that were once considered a part of the nonaligned world, as the 1972 Georgetown Conference of socalled nonaligned nations illustrated so conclusively.

But if nonalignment is more difficult and neutralism passé, the alliances of the multipolar period are less demanding in general than were those of the bipolar age. It is now entirely possible to engage in alliances without losing one's flexibility or independence of action on a wide range of other fronts. The old insistence upon a completely binding relationship is gone, partly because it is no longer logical, given the power configurations of the present.

In the most fundamental sense, therefore, the new era provides broader political opportunities for most states, large and small. All signs point to a period of intense negotiations. This means that each party will seek to maximize its bargaining strength, displaying its military capacities in some cases, relying upon its allies in others, seeking to portray its internal political cohesion and economic capabilities in the strongest possible light, and not hesitating in efforts to influence the internal politics of its opponents if that is feasible.

111

It must be reiterated that the line between domestic and international politics has never been more indistinct, their interrelation never more intimate. In this respect, the open and quasi-open societies must bargain under certain handicaps when they deal with rigidly authoritarian regimes. The former are more available both to internal dissidence and to penetration from without. External forces can more easily play upon the elements of doubt and division within them and, on occasion, turn portions of the political elite, the media and other opinion makers to their service. Thus, military capacity alone can never be a full measure of a given society's power in bargaining or conflict situations. We are only beginning to fathom the varied role of the internal cultural-political factor, or that of the international communications factor in an age when the sociopolitical systems characterizing societies differ so markedly.

To what extent can power be forwarded sheerly by economic means? It has recently been argued that if we are moving into an era when the major societies will be able to avoid war, the role of economic power in the international arena will loom increasingly large. Thus, it is submitted, Japan and the countries of West Europe may be able to protect and advance their national interests without the need for costly military expenditures, or even political alliances. There can be little doubt that both Japan and members of the European Community have turned their economic strength to good advantage in recent years. Indeed Japan has achieved, simply through economic power, many of the goals for which it sacrificed so much in vain in the 1930-1945 era. Even in its relations with the two superpowers and with China, its economic capacities represent bargaining leverage of formidable proportions. It would appear unwarranted, however, to push too far the thesis that economic primacy can eliminate the need for other forms of power. In the first place, economic leverage against Communist states has limits easily reached, given the nature of statist economic systems and the alternatives which such states can pursue. Even in relations with other open, "advanced" societies, Japan has discovered the sharp political and economic repercussions that follow from economic advances that are considered too rapid or based upon unfair tactics. Economic nationalism is a weapon easy to apply in response to the extensive use of economic power.

In addition, it is difficult to envisage a situation where issues will not arise—be they issues of territory, equity, or market access—that require a fuller range of bargaining instrumentalities. One such issue relating to Japan has already been noted. When Foreign Minister Fukuda announced in early 1972 that Japan would patrol the Senkaku Islands to protect them against unwarranted seizure (by either Chinese Nationalists or Communists), he was providing a graphic illustration of this point.

In sum, the period we have labelled multipolar contains a number of interesting paradoxes. Power in its various forms and combinations is both increasingly concentrated and more broadly dispersed. The military capacities of the two superpowers are so huge as to defy the imagination, and go far beyond those of any other state. Yet almost everywhere, there has been a rapid proliferation of military power, including the introduction of very modern, highly deadly conventional weapons to states considered third- and fourth-rate powers. The global patterns of economic growth continue in such a fashion as to widen the gap between haves and have-nots, a gap that is often referred to (not completely accurately) as the North-South gap. The world's leading producer nations now have a phenomenal capacity for mass production But in this field also, productive techniques are being widely disseminated, and satisfactory, even highly successful, growth rates are displayed in a growing number of states.

In the political realm also, elements of paradox abound, as centrifugal and centripetal tendencies compete. On the one hand, nationalism remains the dominant political expression of our times and indeed, for many "emerging" states, just embarked on their nation-building process, the nationalist zenith still lies ahead. Even in some of the older states, centralization continues apace, the product of economic planning, an ever keener recognition of the power implicit in a mobilized, activated citizenry, and the capacities of an elite employing modern communications to their fullest. When mass mobilization is conducted efficiently, it produces a tremendous power, available for whatever purposes the state directs and seldom tolerant of doubters or deviationists. On the other hand, in certain advanced states, a reaction against centralization has emerged, flying not internationalist but rather communal or localist banners. In such societies—some of them, like the United States, approaching the frontiers of total freedom—sub-national identifications appear once again to be gaining strength, and mass mobilization on a national scale seems politically impossible. As if turning back full cycle, the iconoclasts of the post-modern society seek the restoration of primordial ties and, in this, they find an identification with the more "primitive" societies of our times.

The coexistence of these contradictory political trends may prove to be the single most important influence of the late twentieth century on the nature and application of power in international relations.

Summary: Policy Implications in Asia. Let us now try to apply some of the above themes to policy alternatives in the Pacific-Asian area. The United States has long been criticized for having had no coordinated Asian policy. The criticism has some merit. It is a mistake to develop a policy toward one country or region without reference to its repercussions elsewhere, as the U.S. has often tried to do. On the other hand, Asia cannot be treated as a unit either, by any major power. As we have seen, this vast, heterogenous area, covering nearly half of the world, contains a number of reasonably discrete regions, each with its own set of unique problems and relationships. For every important state of the area, the arduous task of achieving linkage in its Pacific-Asian policies, and thereby rendering them consistent yet flexible, remains the supreme challenge.

Two sets of overarching relations are currently of great importance because they link the various regions of Asia with each other and also Asia with Europe. We have referred to these earlier as the two critical triangles. The U.S.S.R.-U.S.-China triangle, it will be recalled, relates centrally to such issues as peaceful coexistence and weapons control. In the broadest sense, this triangle is relevant to the issue of political-military relations in the nuclear age, but at a point in time when the values and goals of various states remain widely disparate. The Japan-U.S.-West Europe triangle focuses upon economic relations among advanced, open societies, but with deep implications for the rest of the world as well.

The existence and importance of these two sets of triangular relationships gives striking evidence of that element of multipolarity in international affairs to which we and others have paid homage. At the same time, our survey should have underlined the continuing importance to the Pacific-Asian area (and the world) of the two superpowers as entities unto themselves. Notwithstanding recent setbacks in the Middle East, the substantial increase in Soviet power and commitments in Asia might well be considered the most important political development affecting the area during the last decade. This development, moreover,

114

contrasts and coincides with a reduction in American power and commitment toward Asia, and the possibility of an even more comprehensive withdrawal.

These two events have already had substantial internal repercussions in a number of Asian states, as well as in the power structure of certain regions. Their impact would have been greater had it not been for the emergence of a strongly anti-Soviet China, massive if not yet modern. In sum, bipolarism may be fading but it remains significant and should not be ignored.

Another fact of supreme importance characterizes the international relations of this area. Relations among major societies are highly asymmetrical. Indeed, one of the current advantages of the American position in Asia, offsetting to some extent the uncertainties concerning its commitments, is the fact that the United States alone has access to all of the other major states on a basis that makes dialogue, and even substantive agreements, possible. But even in *its* relations, the United States has radically different degrees of interest, involvement and intimacy.

Thus, the concept of an equidistant mutipolarism has no validity in the Pacific-Asian area, and any attempt to translate it into practice would be fraught with danger. The major societies of this region do not have equal sets of interests or relations with each other; they do not hold equally separated positions on matters of ideology, policy or politico-economic structure; and hence they are not in roughly equal positions with respect to how their respective national interests are defined. Consequently, bilateral relations in Asia as elsewhere will remain extremely important. As we have seen, in the major power relationships of the Pacific-Asian area, two bilateral relations now stand out: those between the United States and Japan and those between the Soviet Union and India. Both are subject to various strains; but both seem likely to endure for the foreseeable future, albeit with modifications, because they fulfill important mutual needs. China, on the other hand, is not likely to acquire a relation of this kind with another major power, although it clearly placed its hopes at one point on the Soviet Union and, at a later point and in an entirely different manner, upon Pakistan.

Bilateral relations of importance will certainly not be confined to the major states. Indeed, each of the major states is likely to have a number of such relations with smaller states, differing considerably in character. Multilateral organizations and relationships will thus serve as a supplement, not a substitute for bilateral ties in most instances. The necessity of multilateralism, however, is now as apparent in the political-security field as in the economic arena. Yet we are a very great distance from finding the mechanisms that will make multilateralism in the political-military field sufficiently effective or even sufficiently promising to induce widespread acceptance. The risks of multilateralism remain high, especially in situations where the stakes are crucial. Thus, experimentation, while urgent, must also be cautious. Operative bilateral relations and commitments are likely to be given up in most cases only after a new multilateral system has been tested.

There are a few cases where circumstances may warrant selective risks. We have sought to emphasize the fact that there are major differences among the regions that comprise the Pacific-Asian area. At least one region, Northeast Asia, contains the type of power juxtaposition and issue involvement that makes it both critical and dangerous. Here, commitments will be high, bargaining will be focused upon an accommodation minimally satisfactory to all of those involved, and negotiations will probably be determined by the strength and resolve of the respective parties.

In other regions, power and authority will be unevenly matched, giving one state or group of states a dominant role, or else the issues, while highly important, will be carefully defined in such a fashion as to limit the number of primary contestants. The Pacific region and South Asia fit the first condition, the continental center of Asia the second. The latter region, however, carries great potential dangers for adjacent regions and for the general peace, notwithstanding the presence of only two major competitors. In this sense, it shares certain characteristics with Northeast Asia.

In at least one region, Southeast Asia, the interests and involvement of the major powers may be sufficiently evenly balanced and/or compatible to enable either mutual disengagement or carefully regulated, minimal involvement. Clearly, Southeast Asia's future hinges to some extent upon such a condition.

In any case, the primary task for the major states in certain regions of the Pacific-Asian area is to solve problems, in others to contain them, and in a few situations to ignore them. The task of the smaller states meanwhile is to find the means appropriate to preserving their independence and advancing their economic growth through various combinations of bilateral and multilateral ties, coupled with policies that mix self-reliance and interdependence. In sum, neither for large nor small states is there a single policy route that can suffice for so complex a set of problems and so vast an area. Coordination, not uniformity, is the requirement of the times.

Cover and book design: Pat Taylor